AF477431

Solitudes of Human Places

Edition Patrick Frey № 333

Jong Won Rhee

Solitudes of Human Places

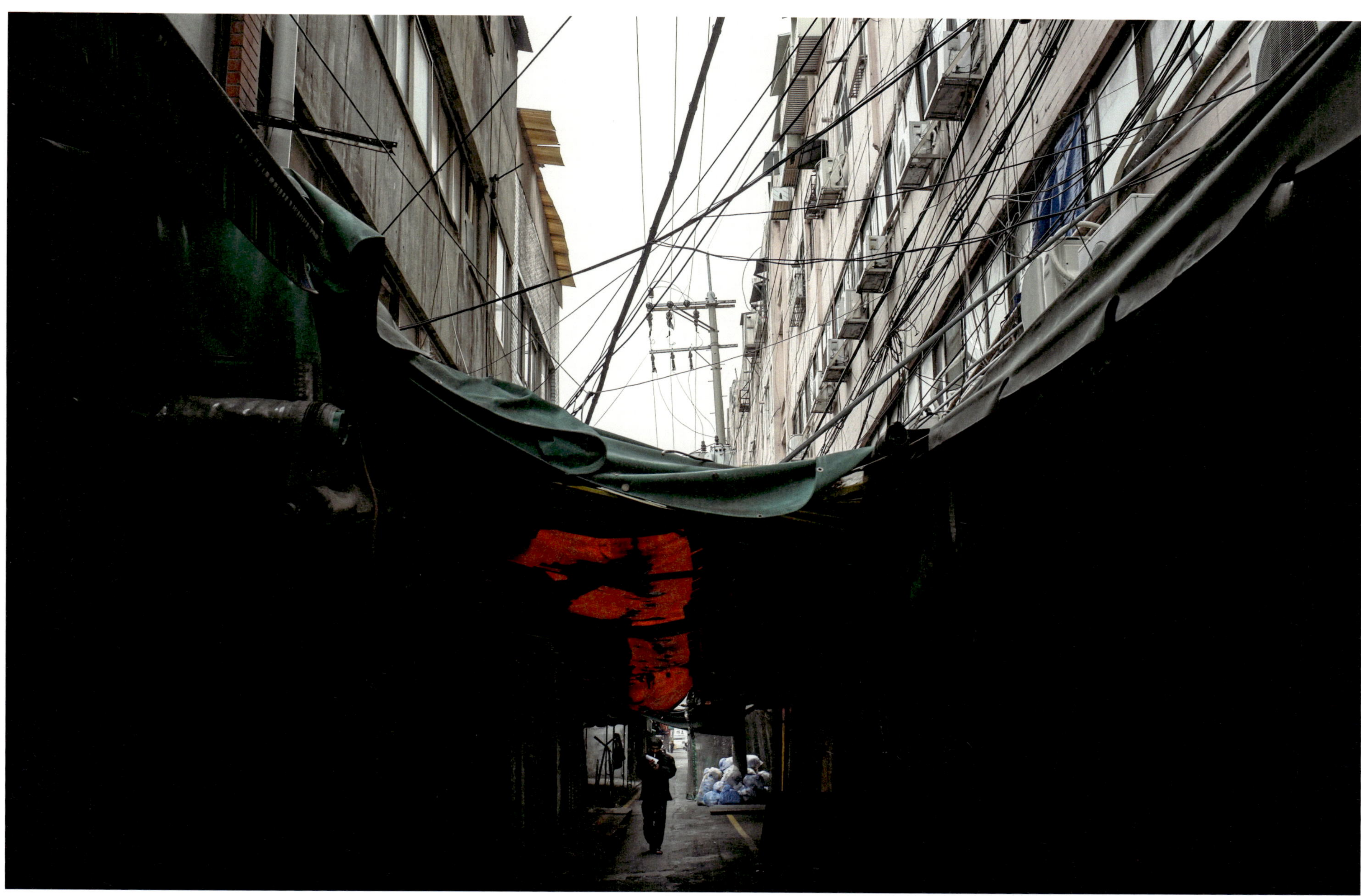

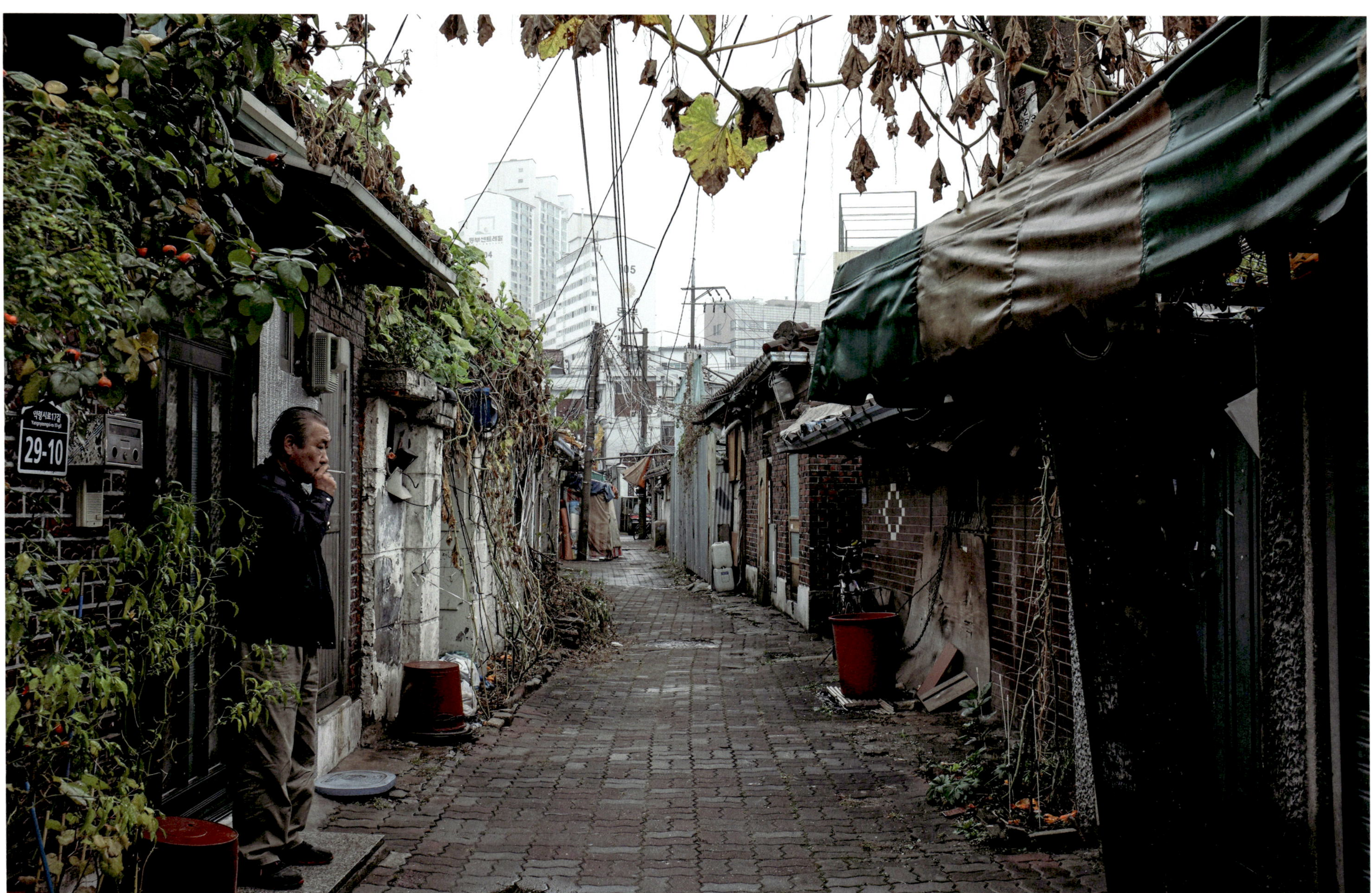

29-10

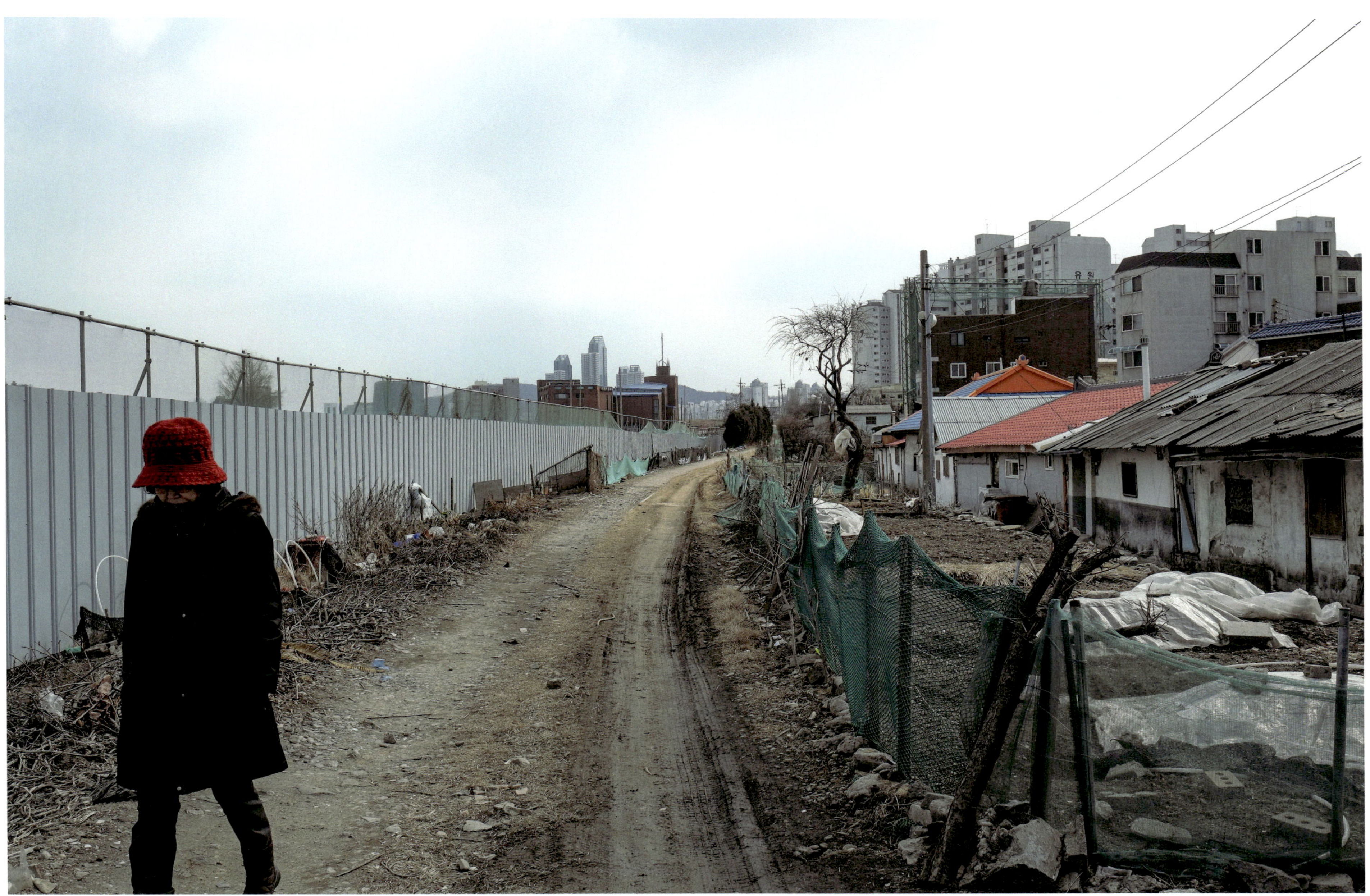

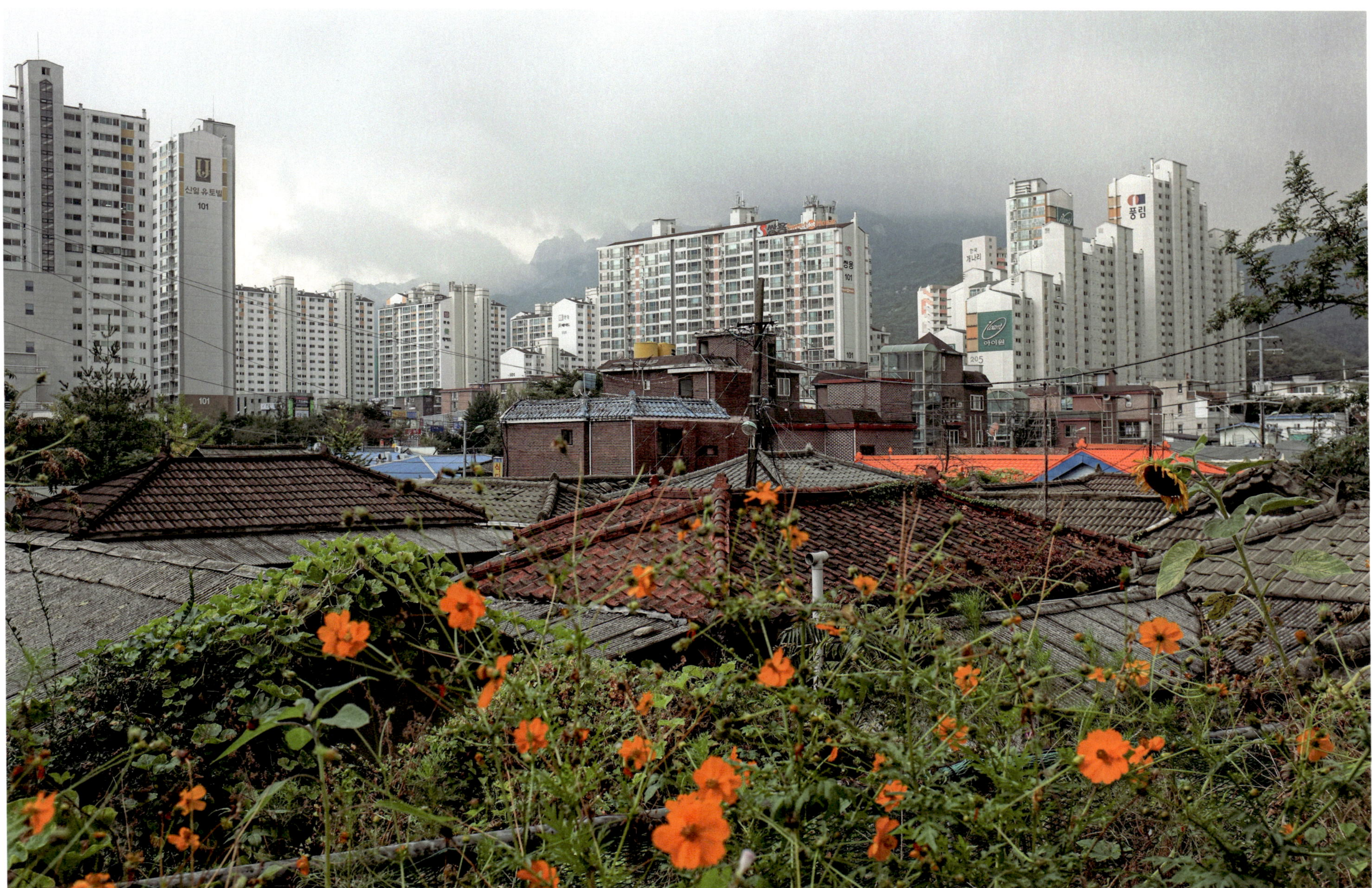

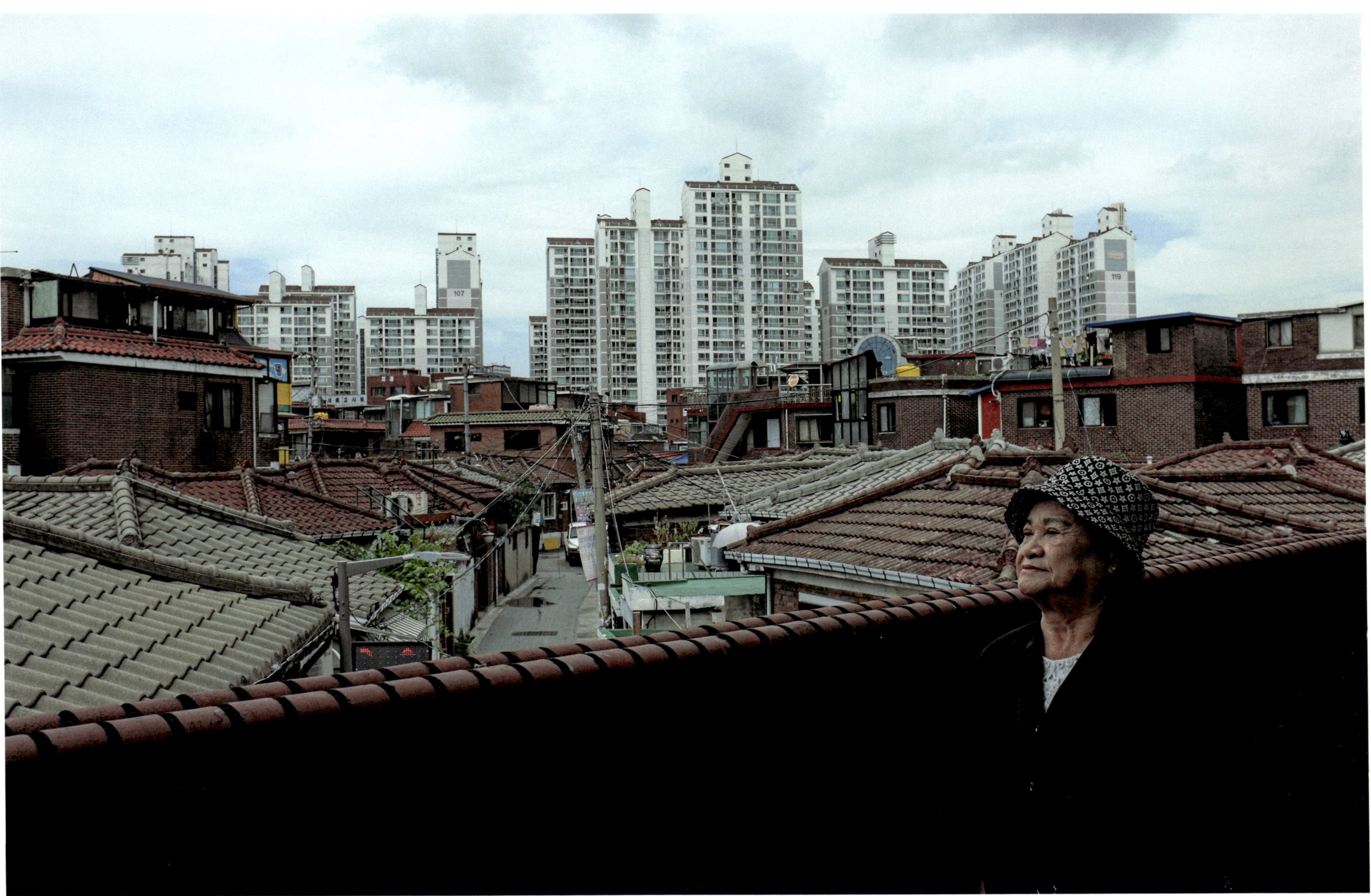

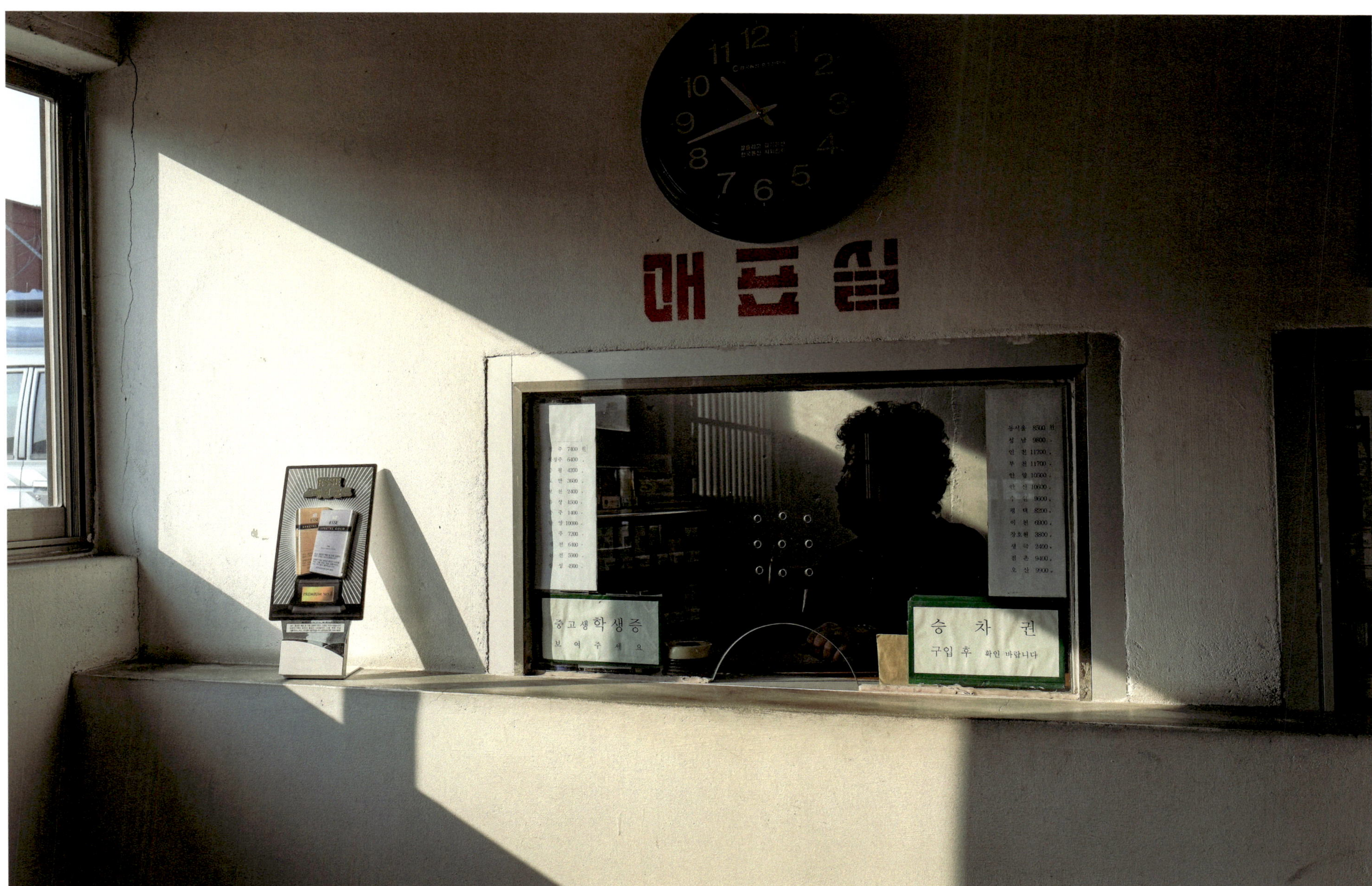

매표실
중고생학생증
보여주세요
승차권
구입 후 확인 바랍니다

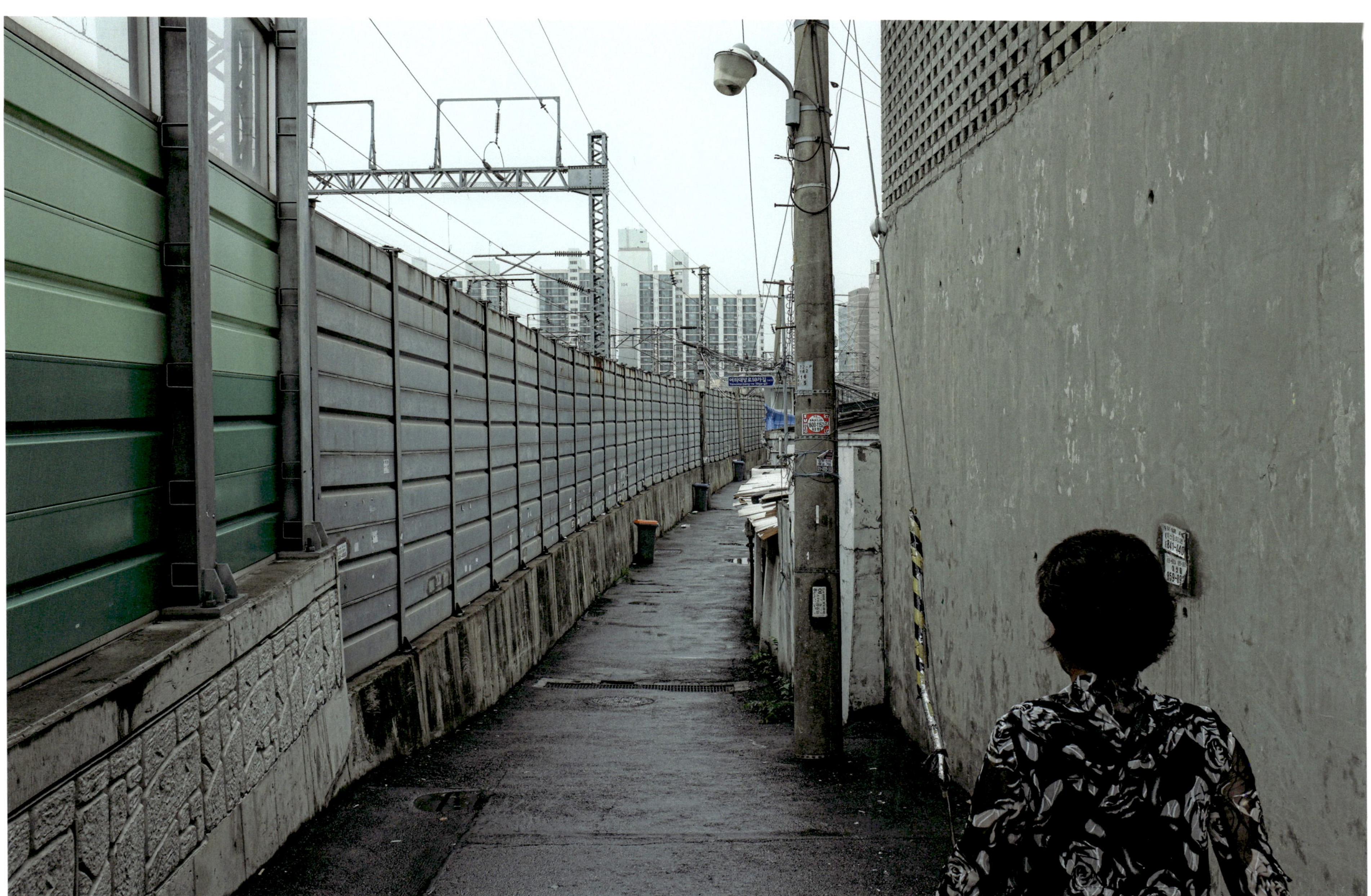

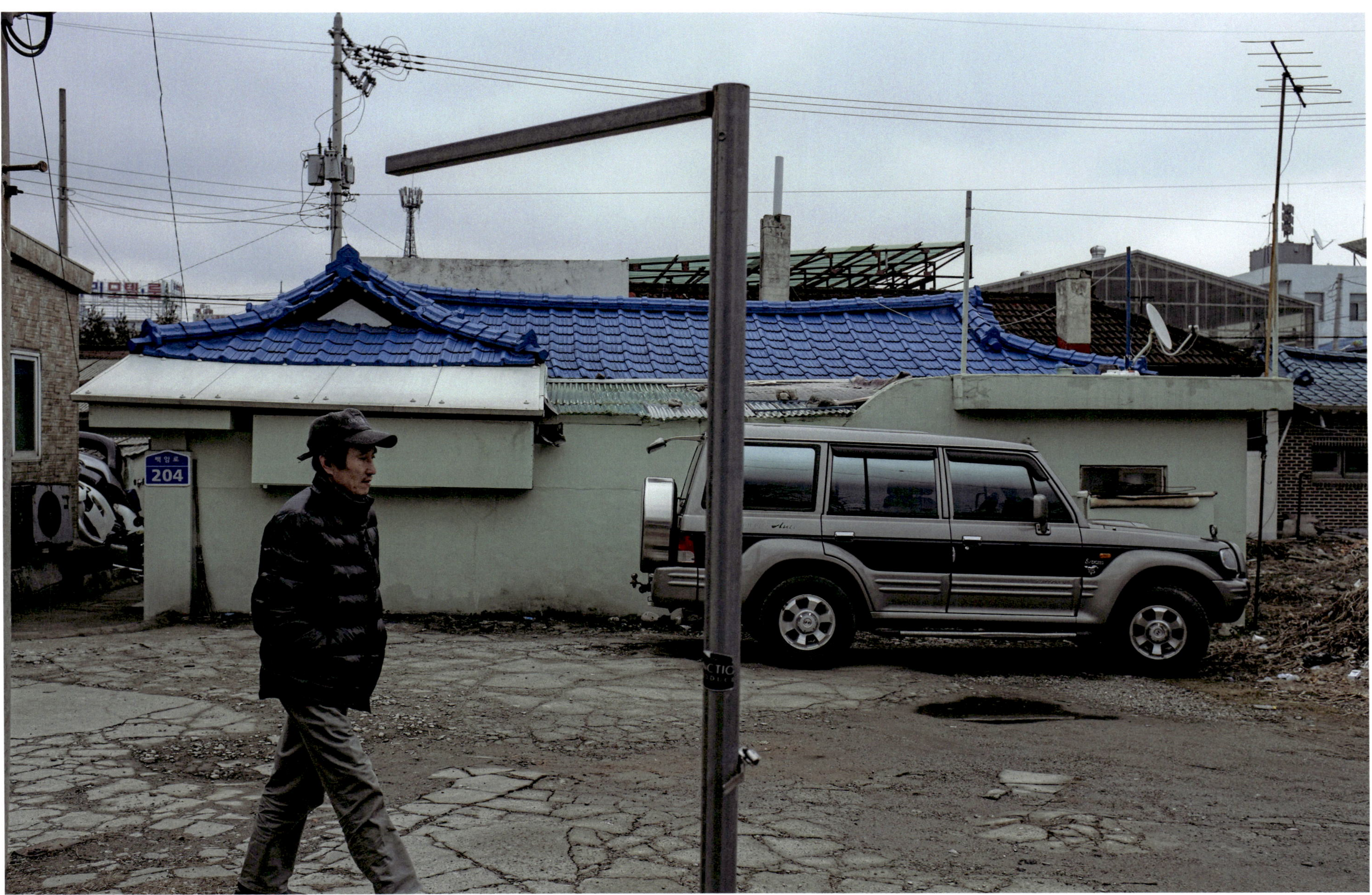
204

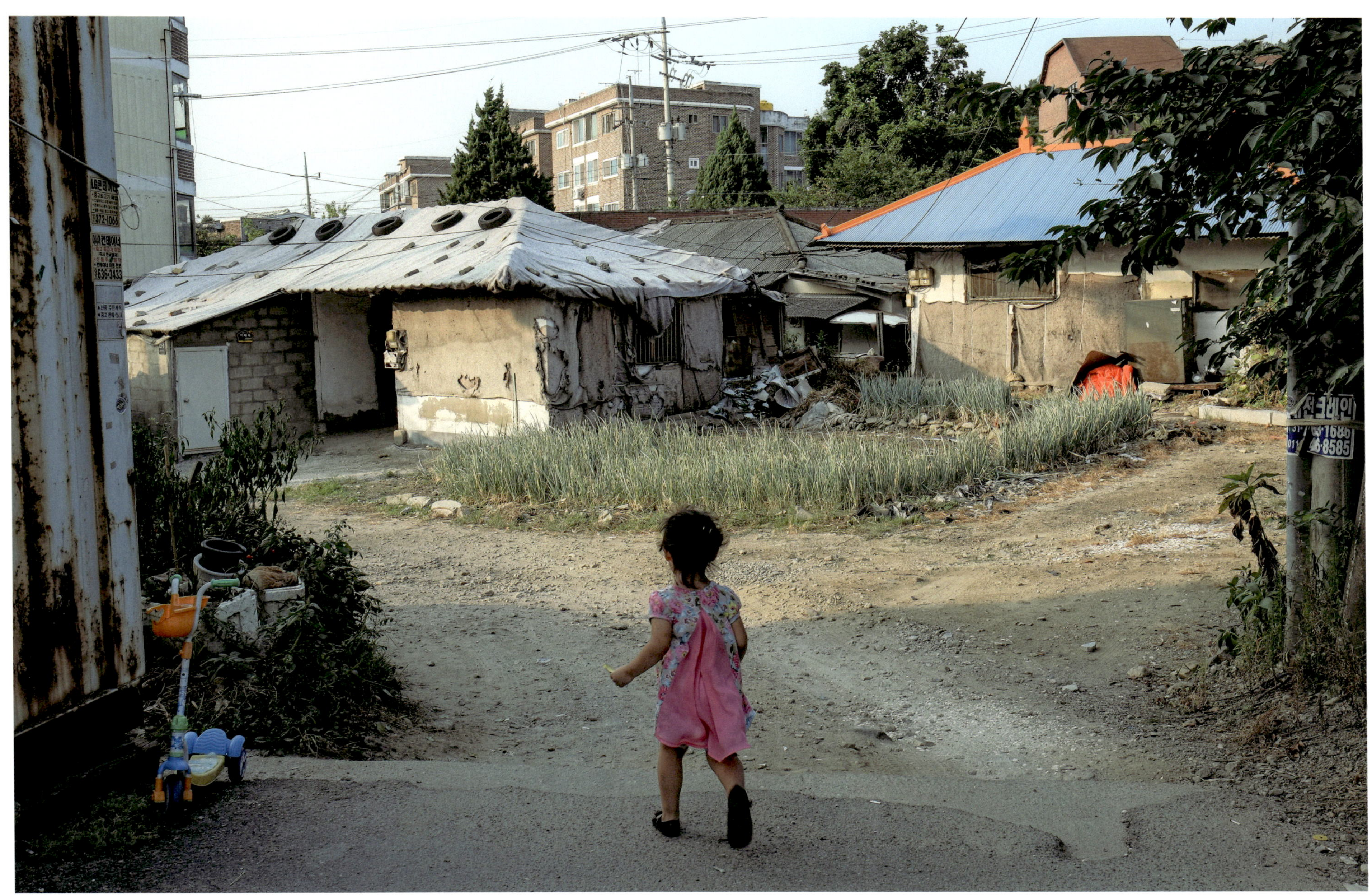

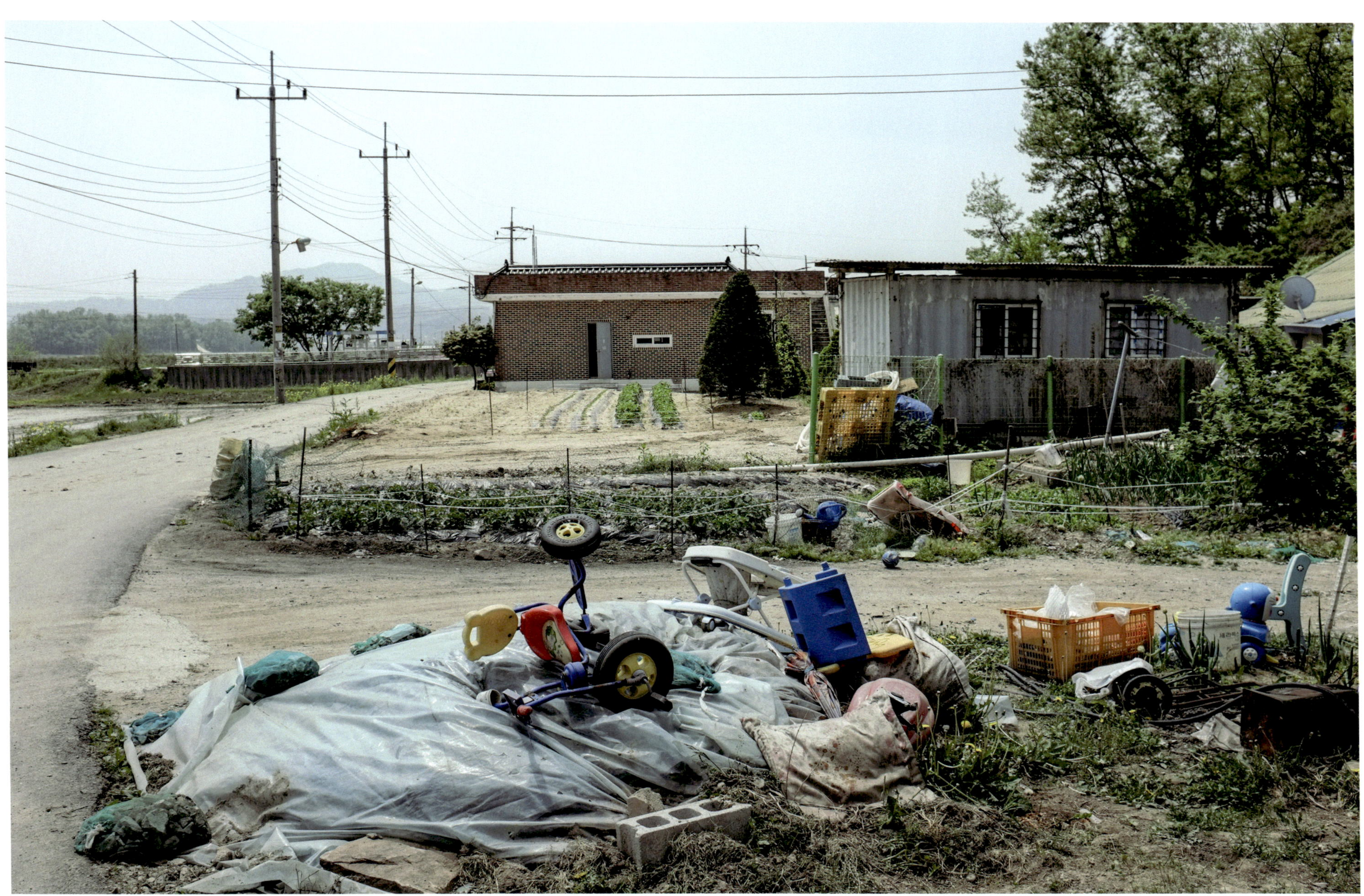

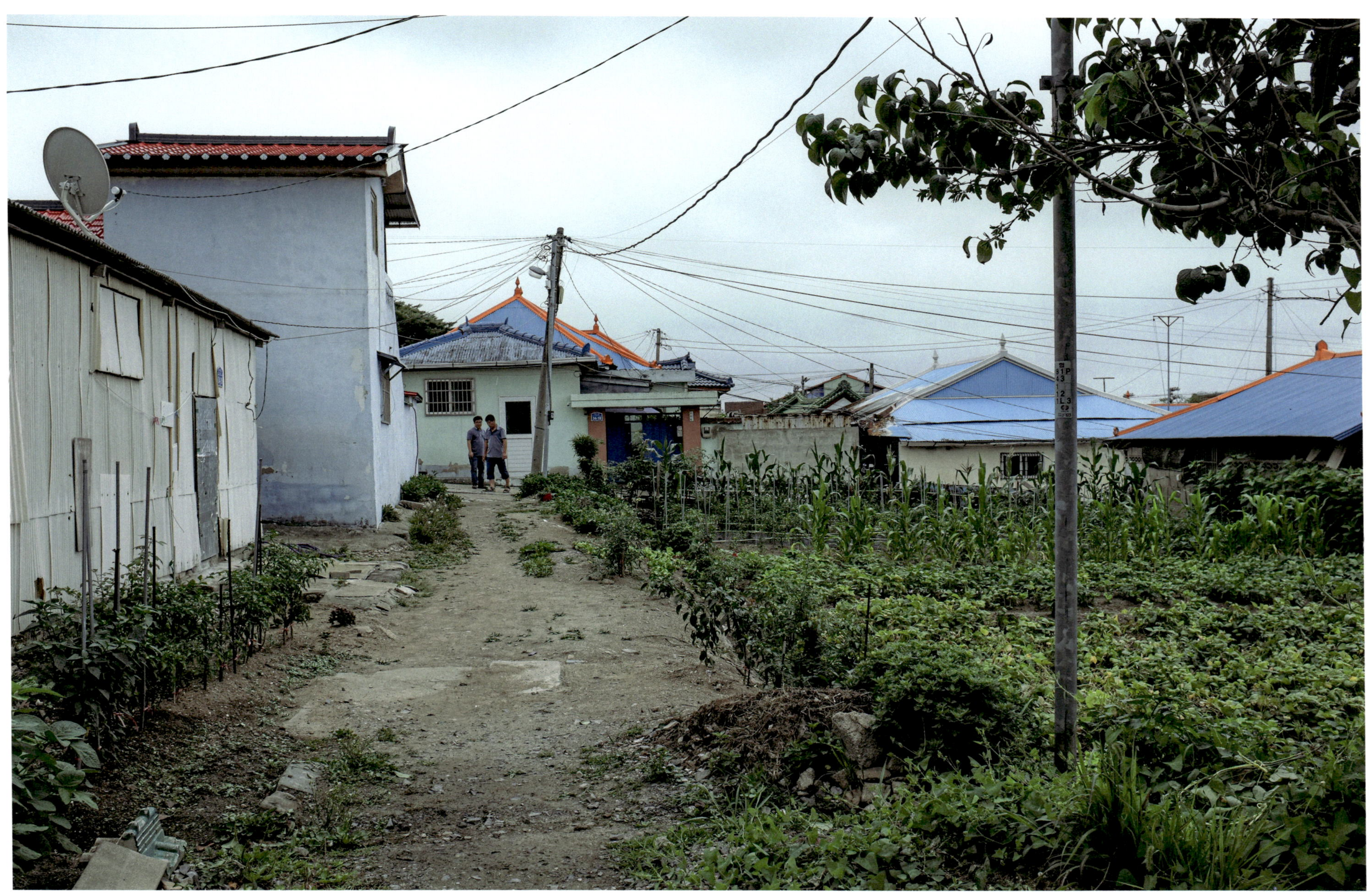

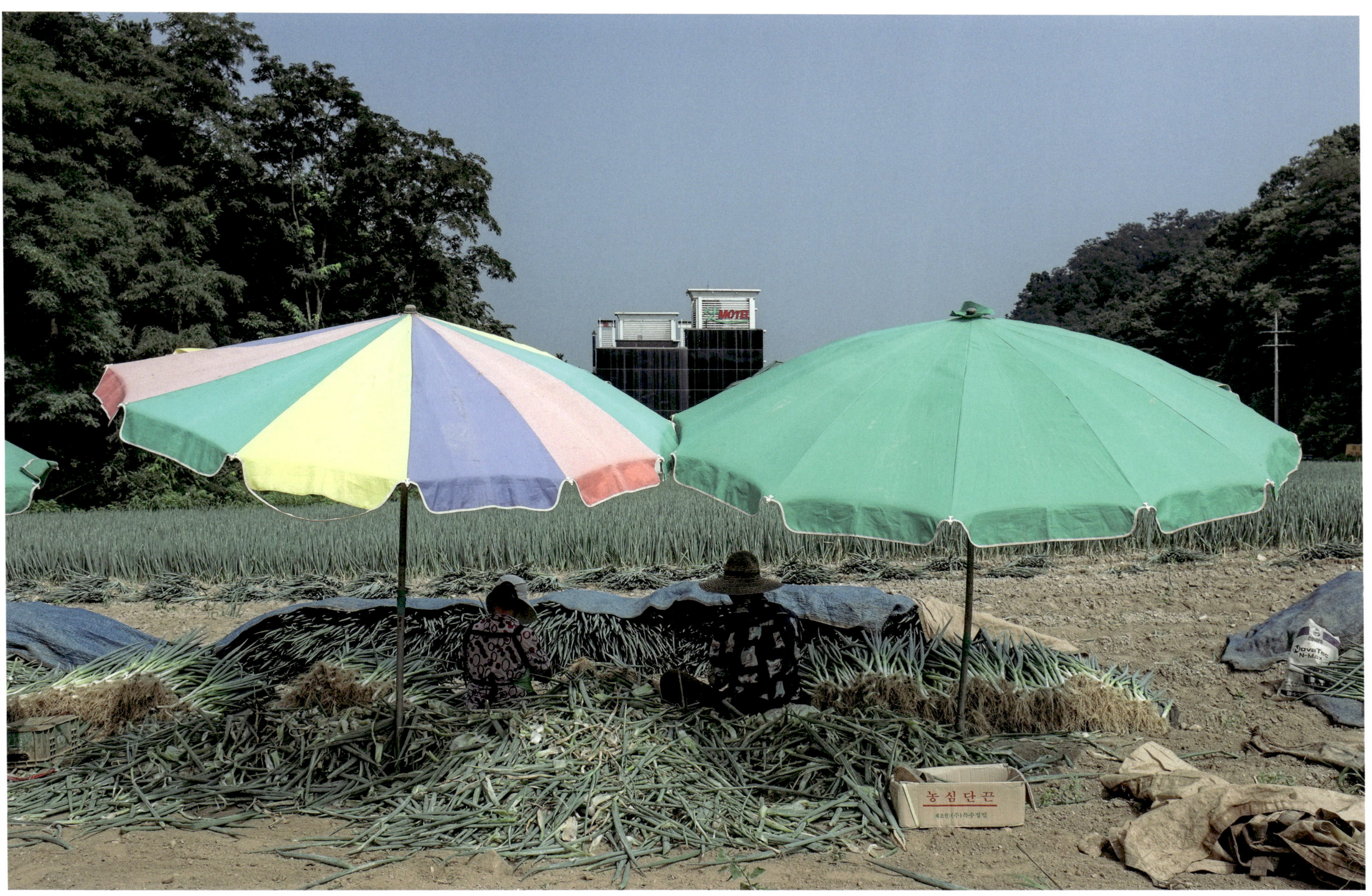
天 MOTEL
농 심 단 끈
제조원:(주)특수

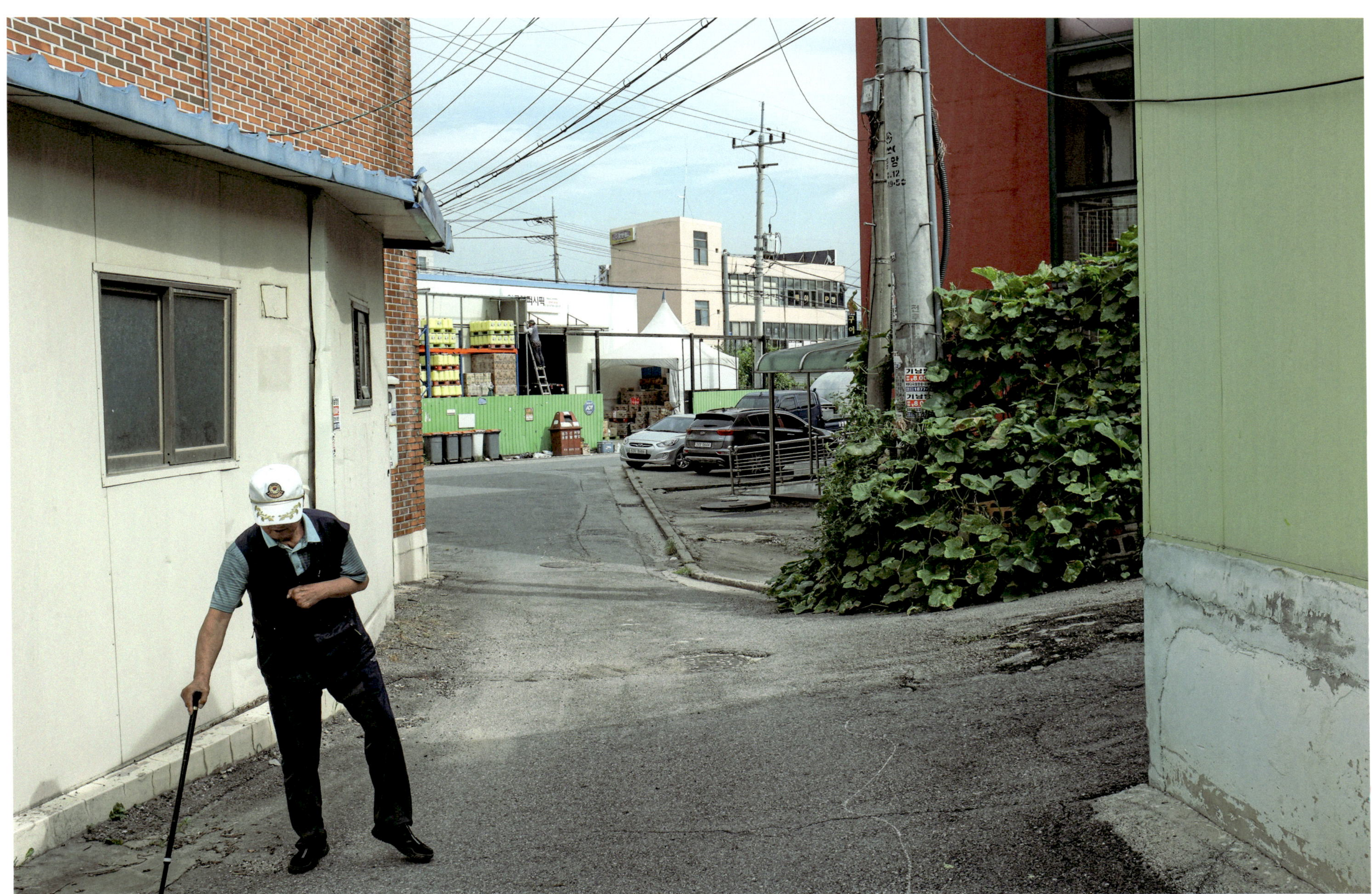

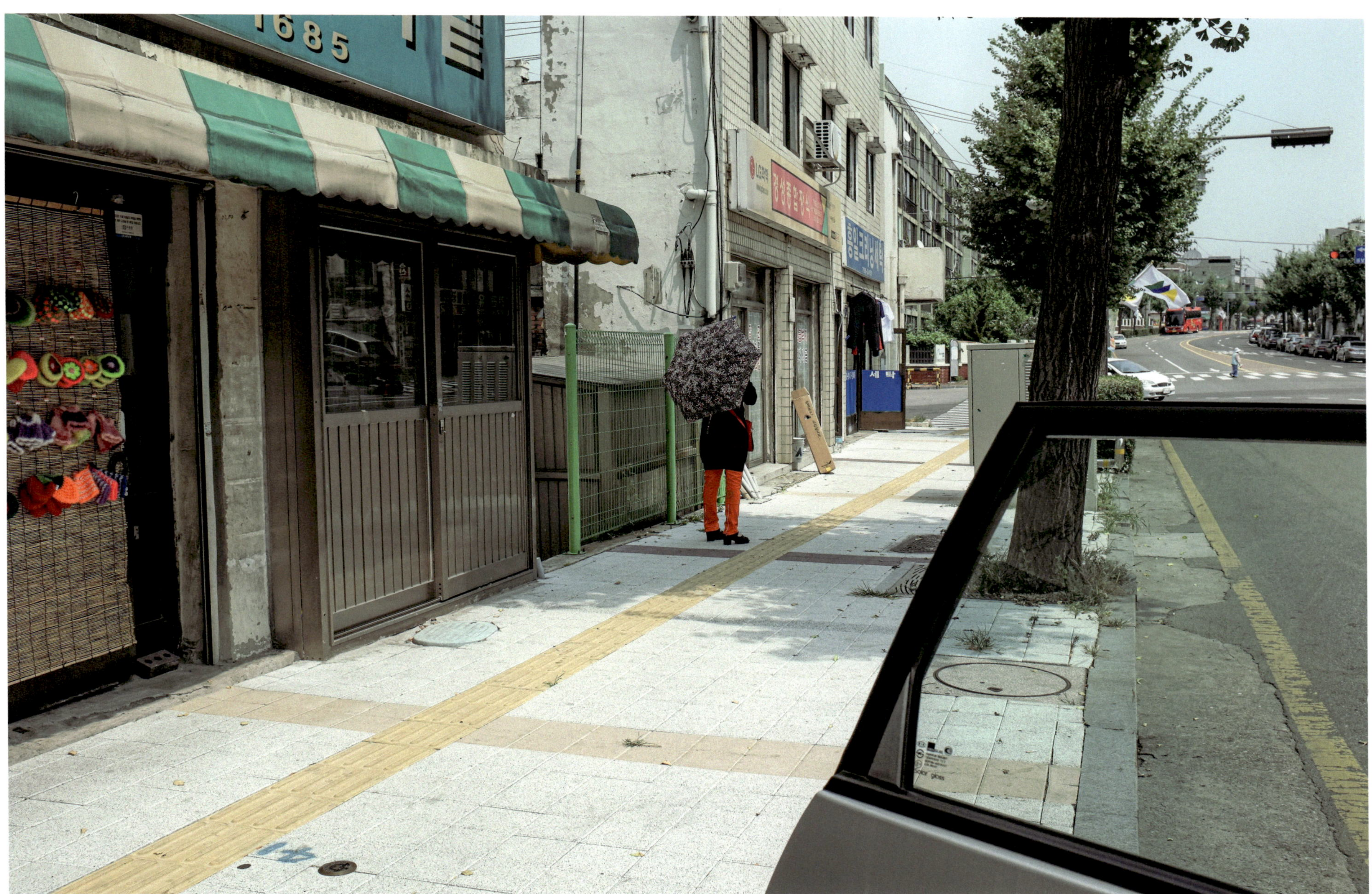

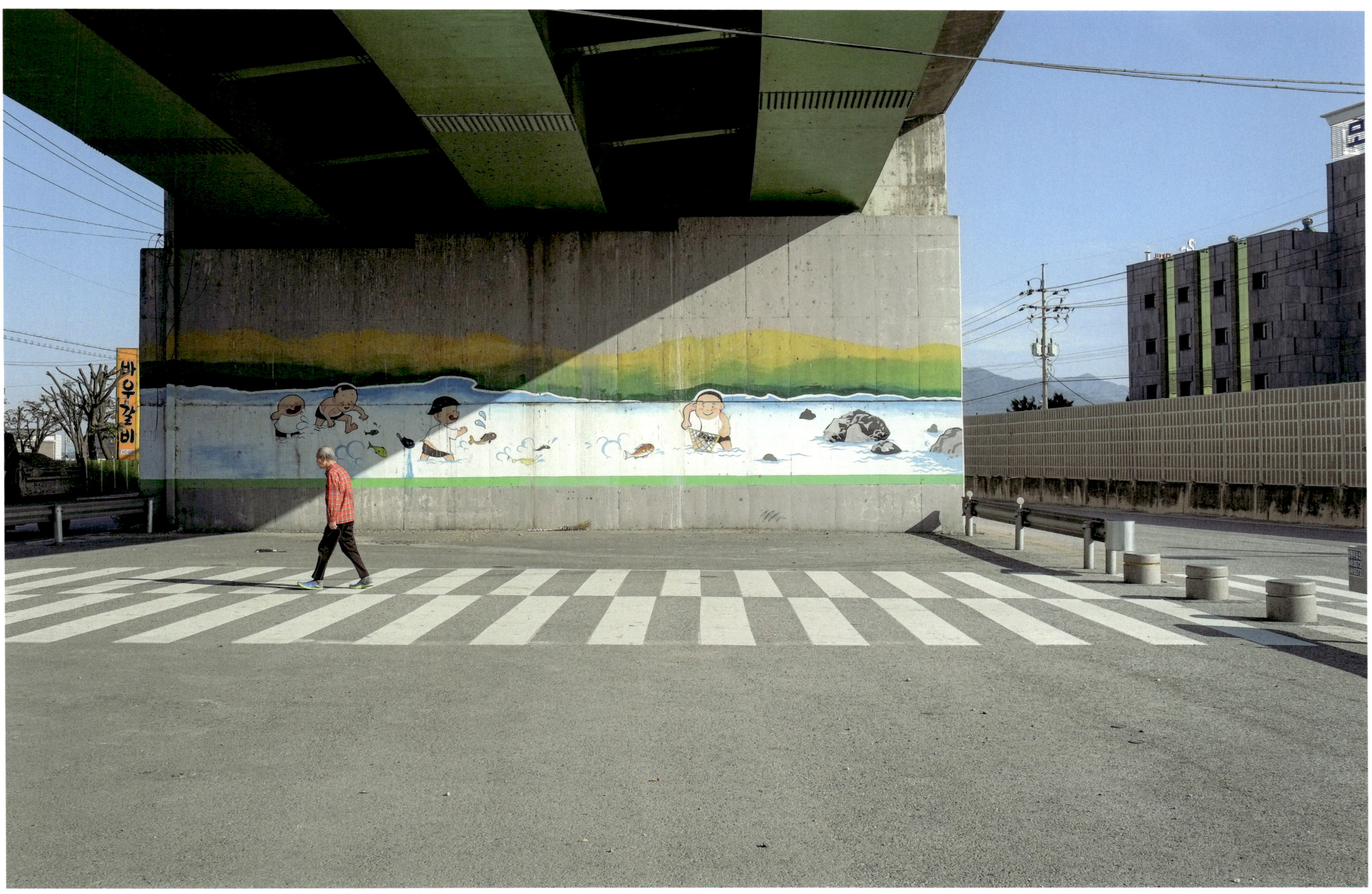

바우갈비

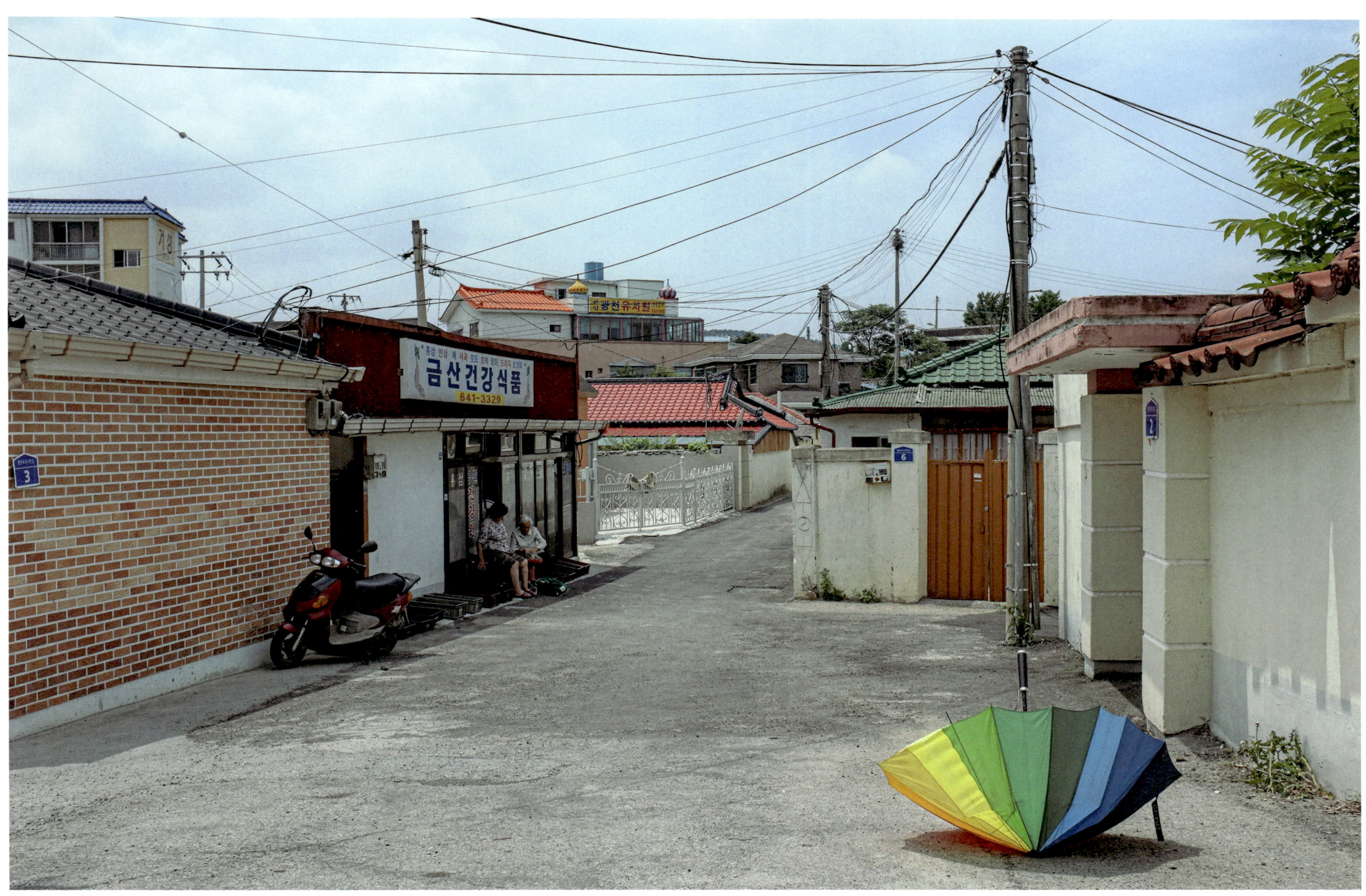
홍삼 인삼 배 사과 포도 호박 양파 도라지 오가피
금산건강식품
641-3329
3
6
2

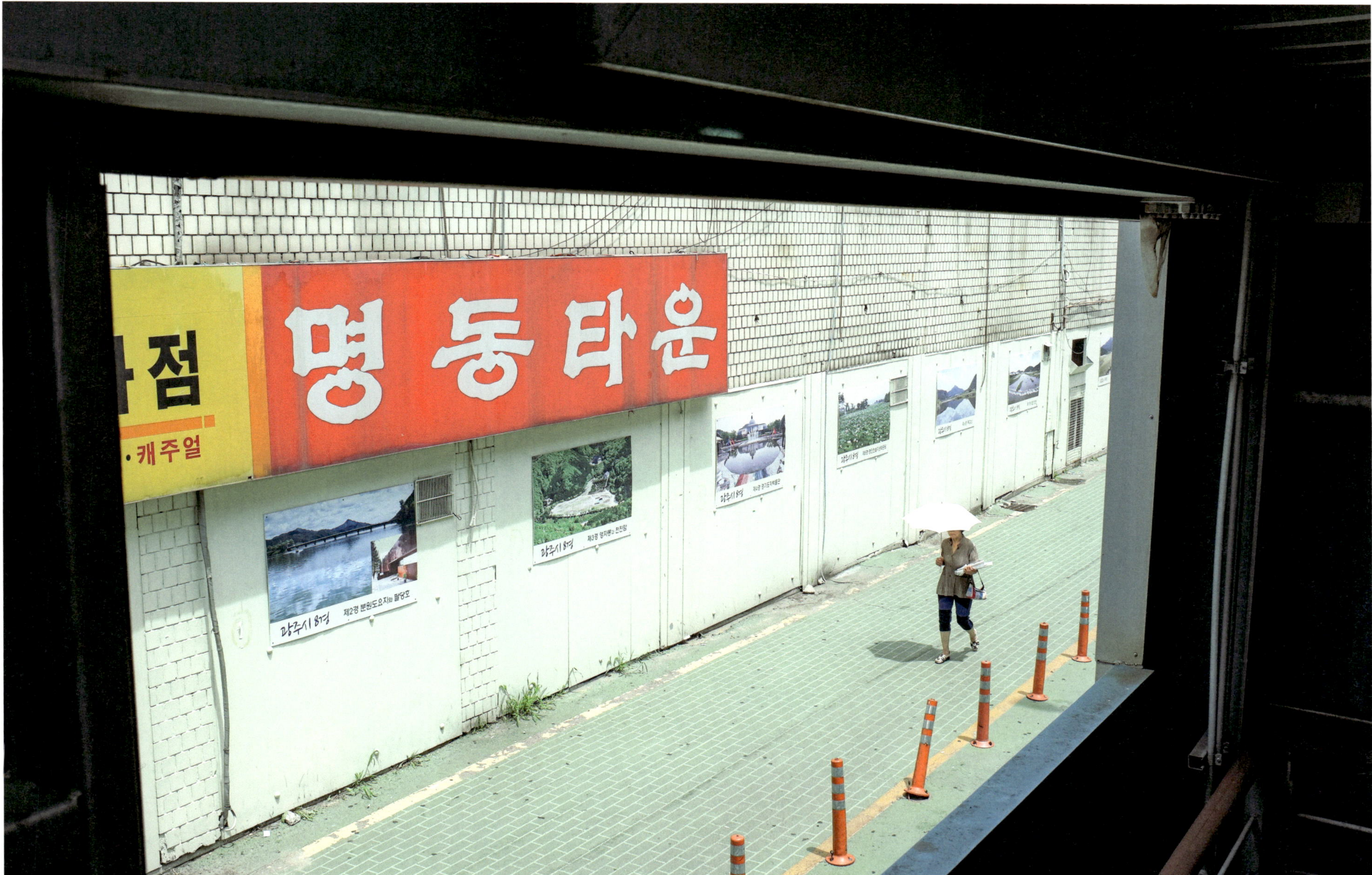
명동타운
점
· 캐주얼
광주시 8경
광주시 8경
광주시 8경
광주시 8경

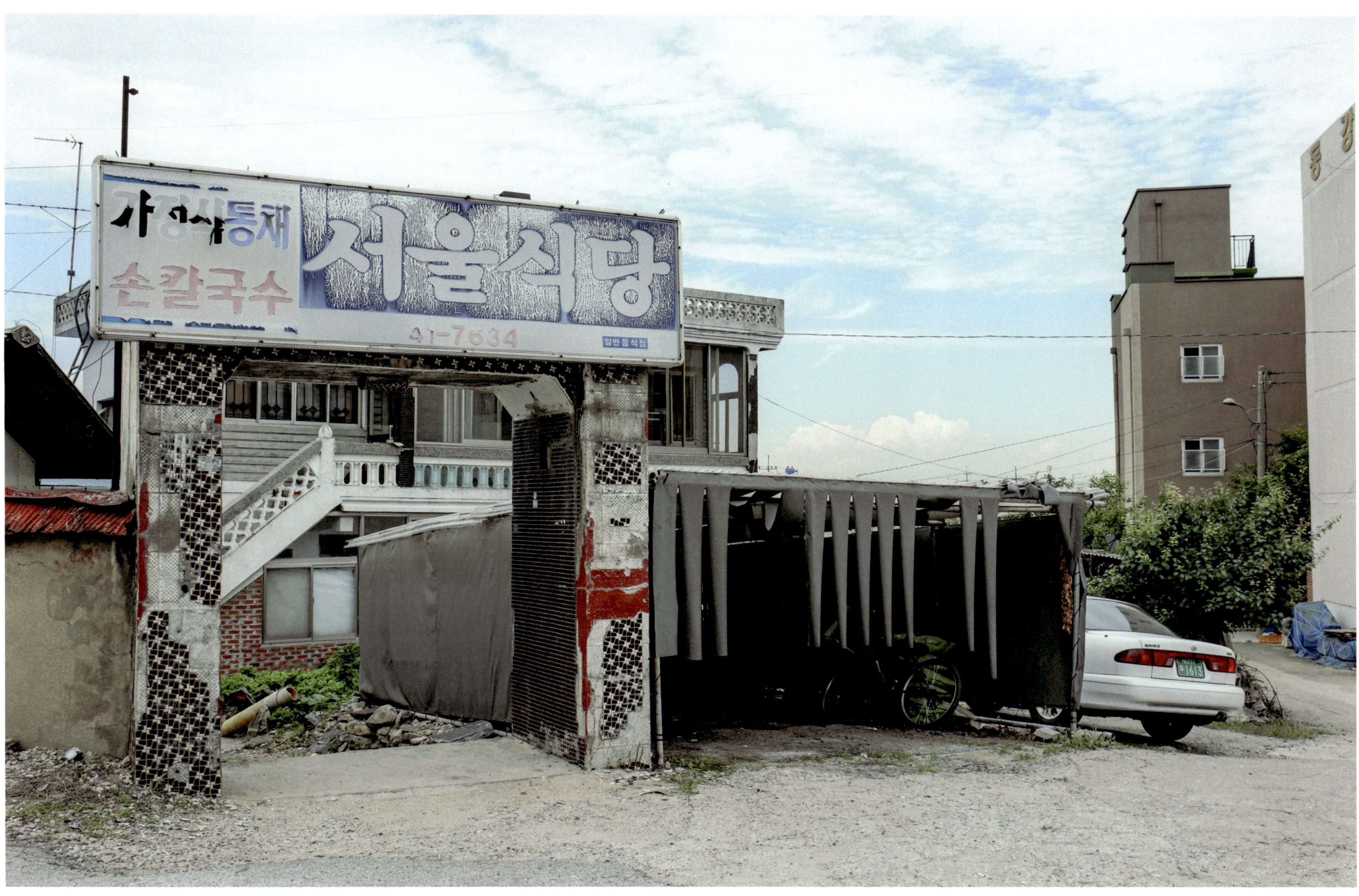
가경시 동채
손칼국수
서울식당
41-7634
일반음식점

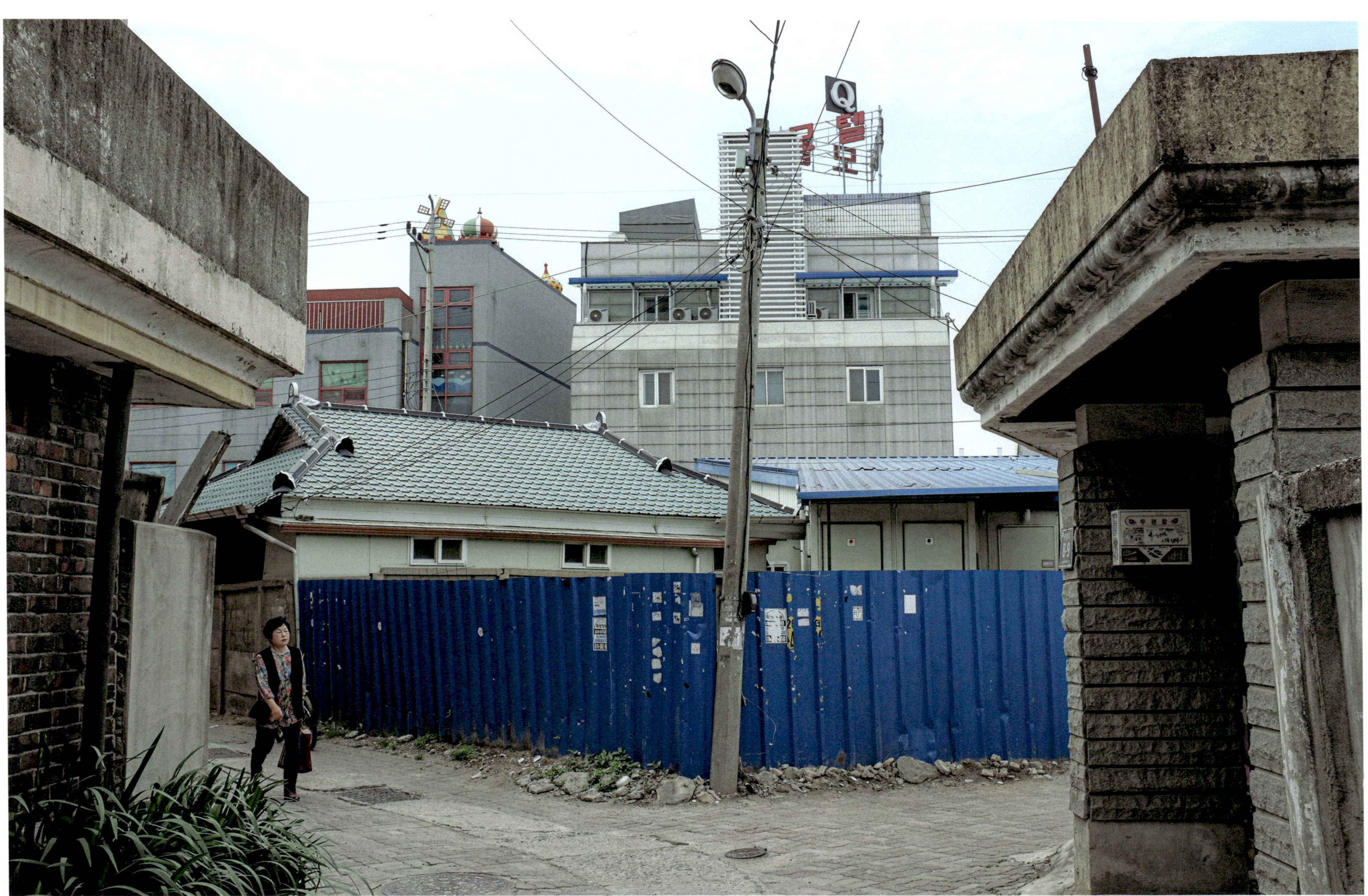

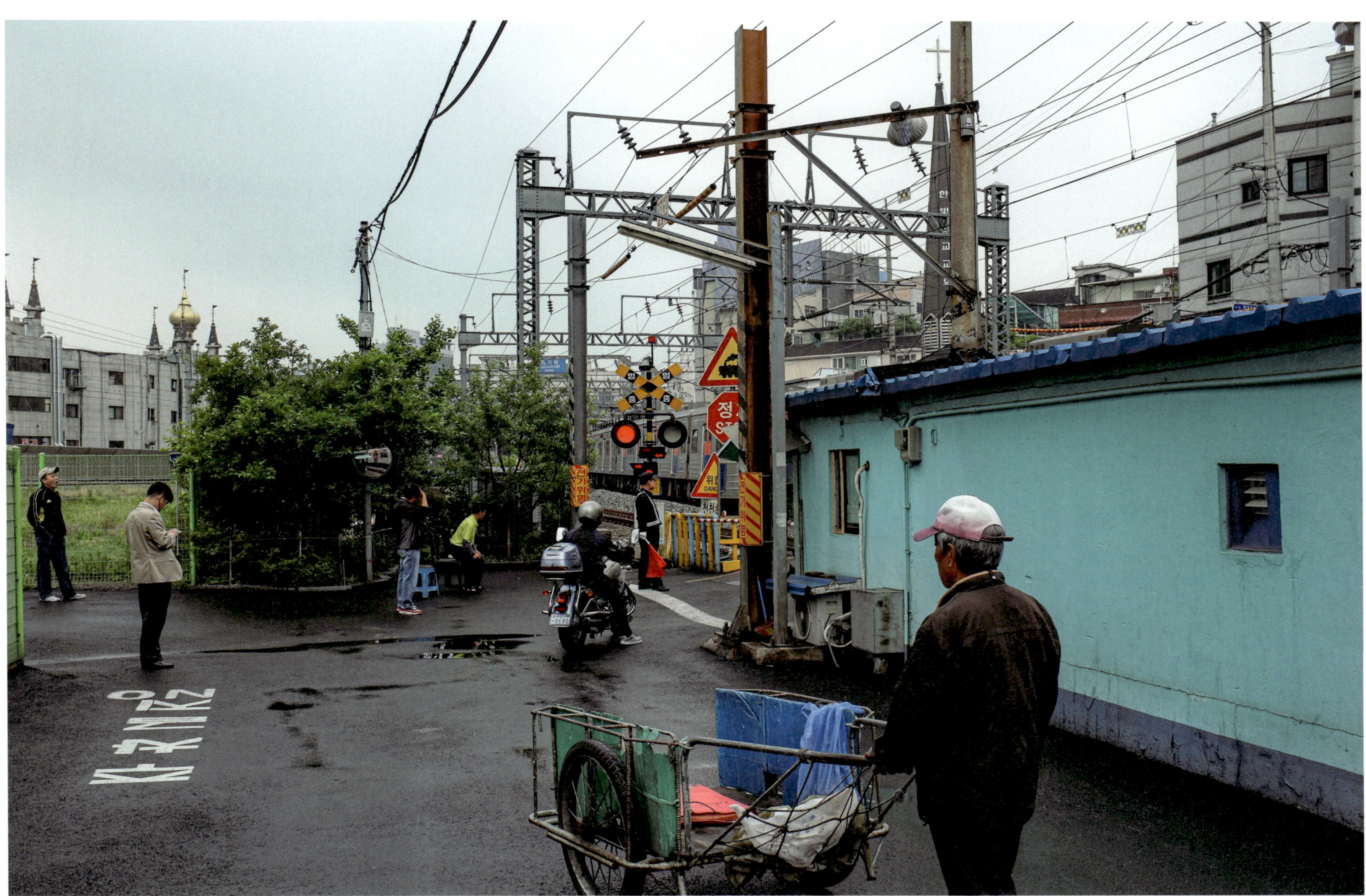

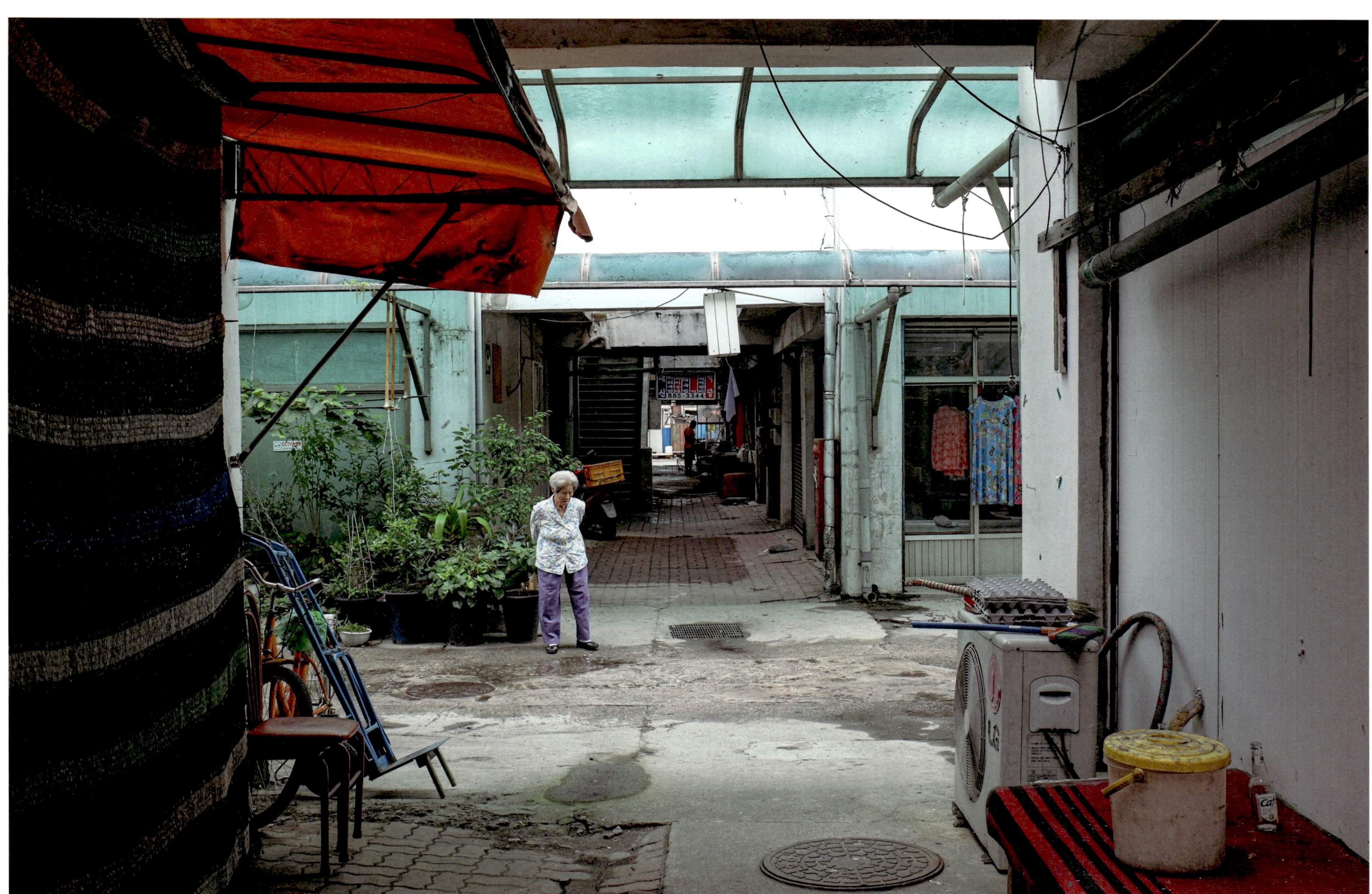

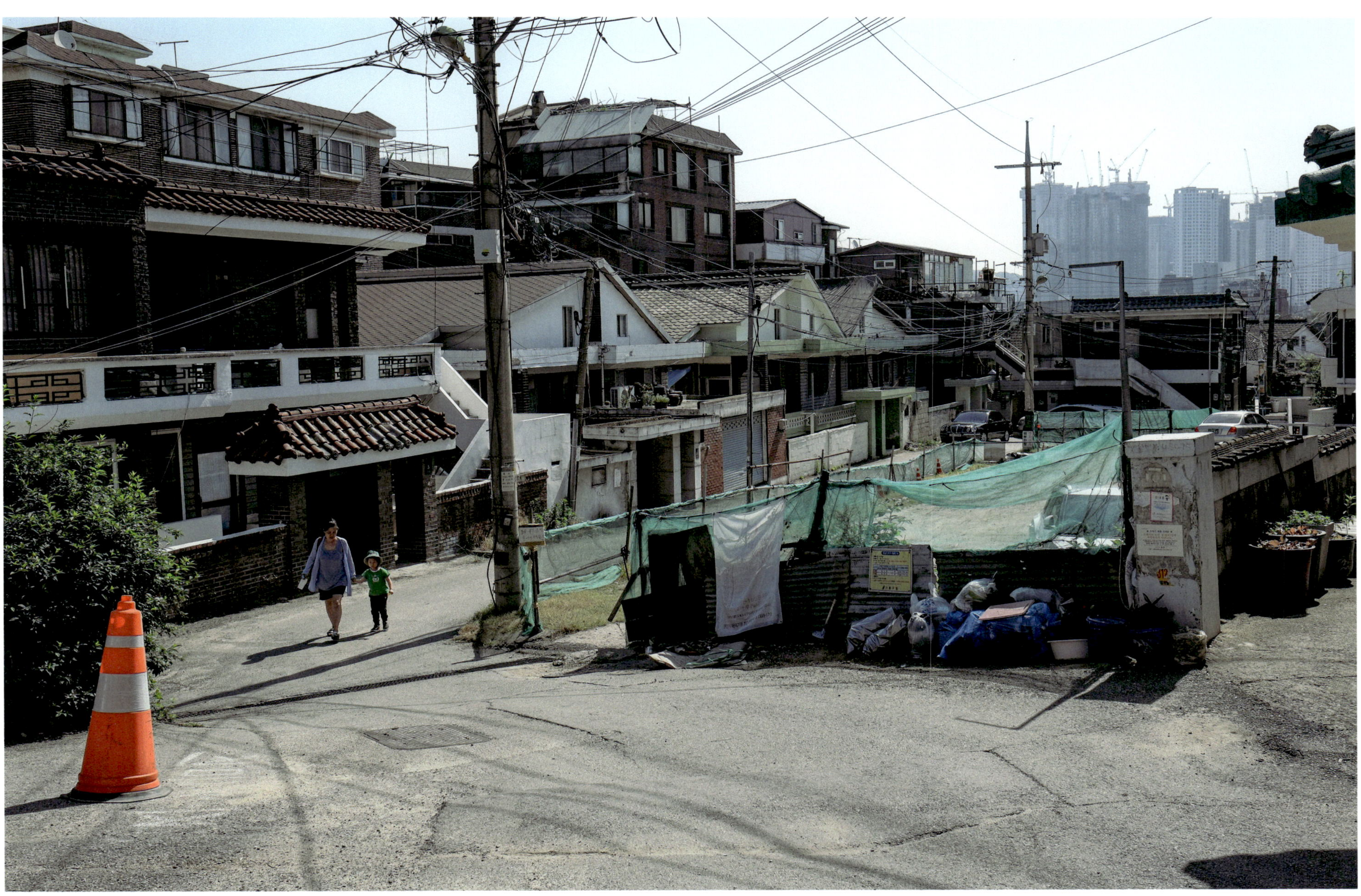

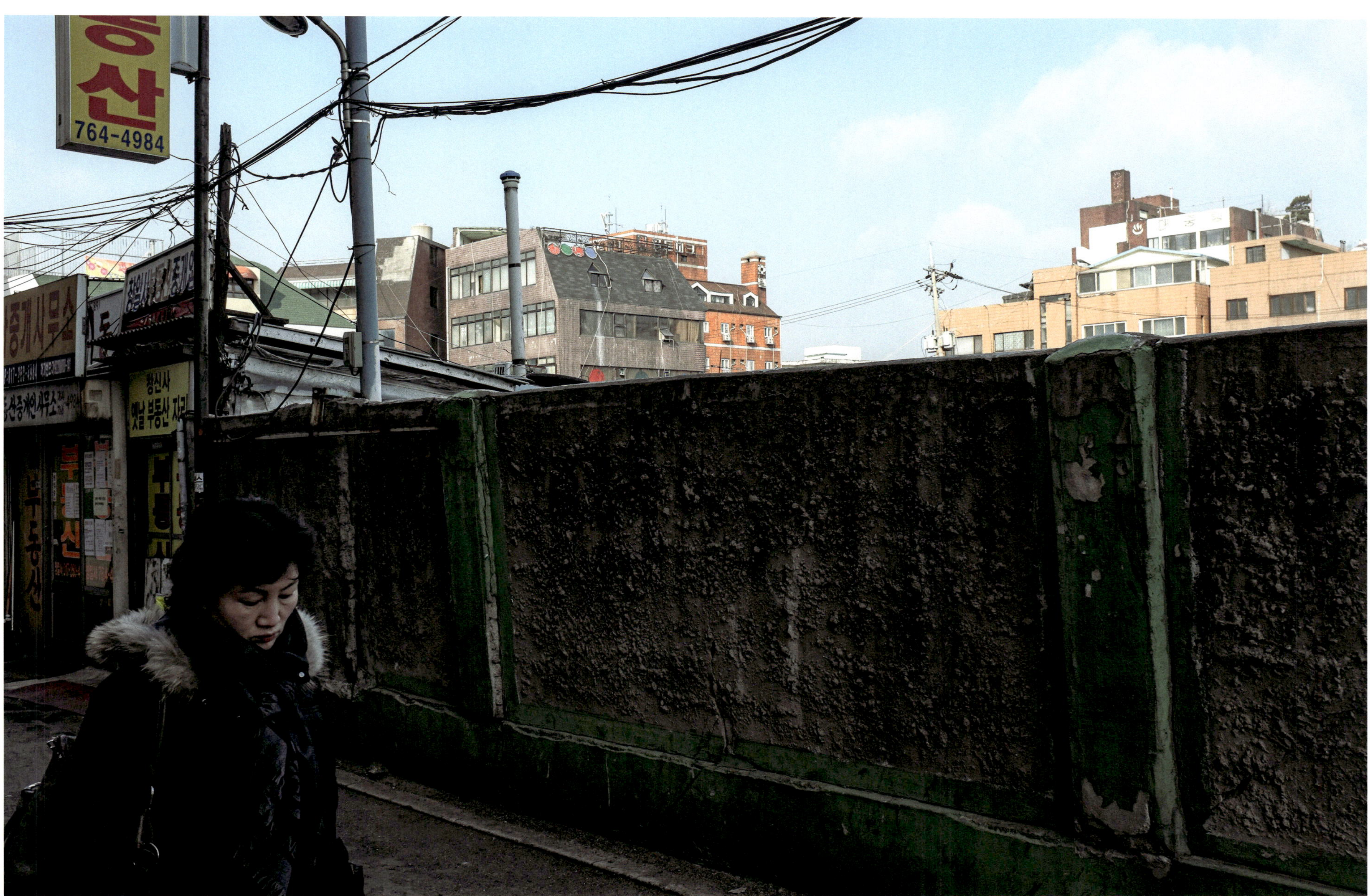
산
764-4984
중개사무소
황신사
옛날 부동산 자리
부동산

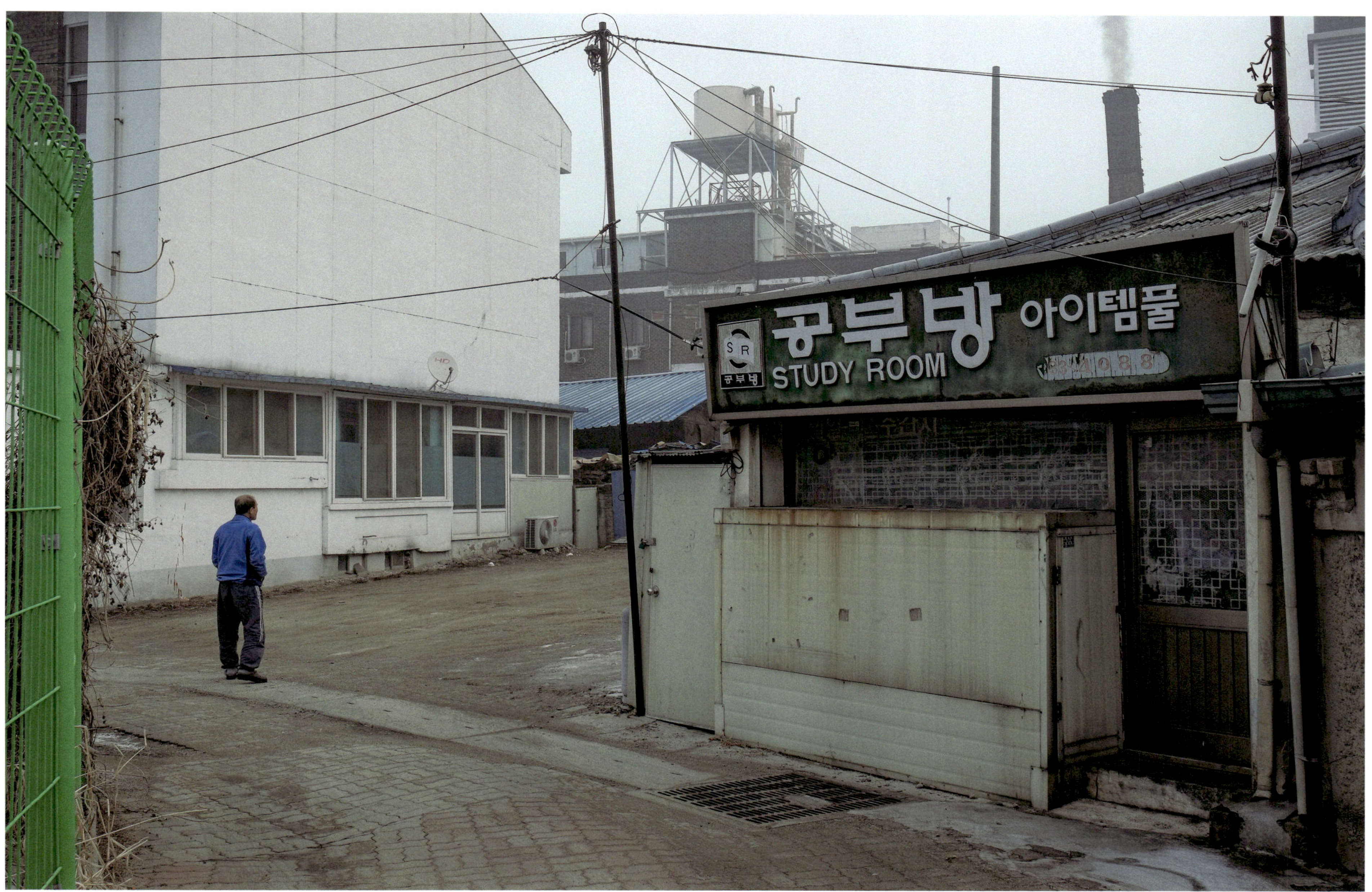

S R 공부넷
공부방 아이템풀
STUDY ROOM

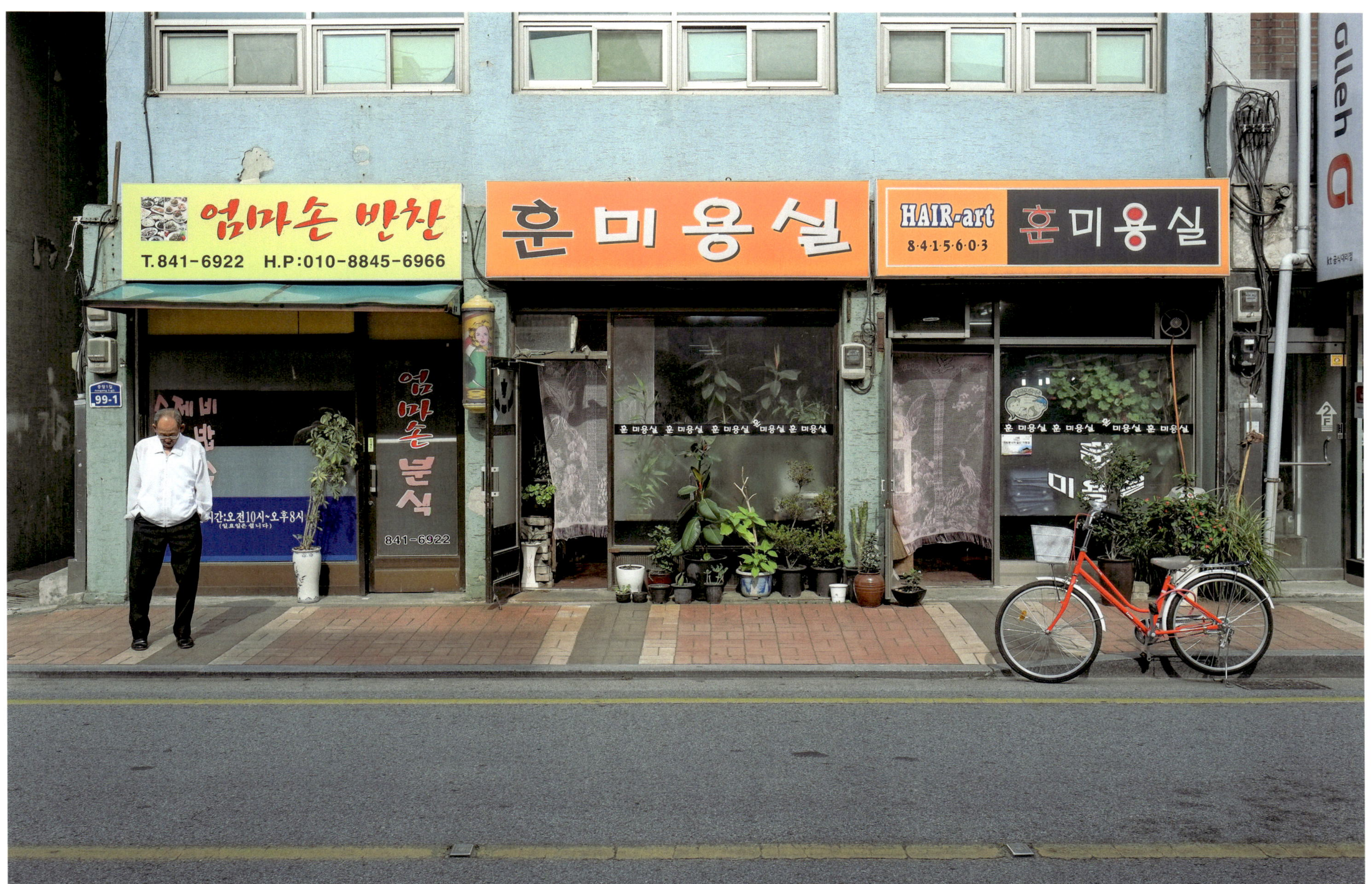

엄마손 반찬
T. 841-6922   H.P:010-8845-6966
엄마손 분식
841-6922
훈 미용실
HAIR-art
8·4·1·5·6·0·3
훈 미용실
olleh
99-1

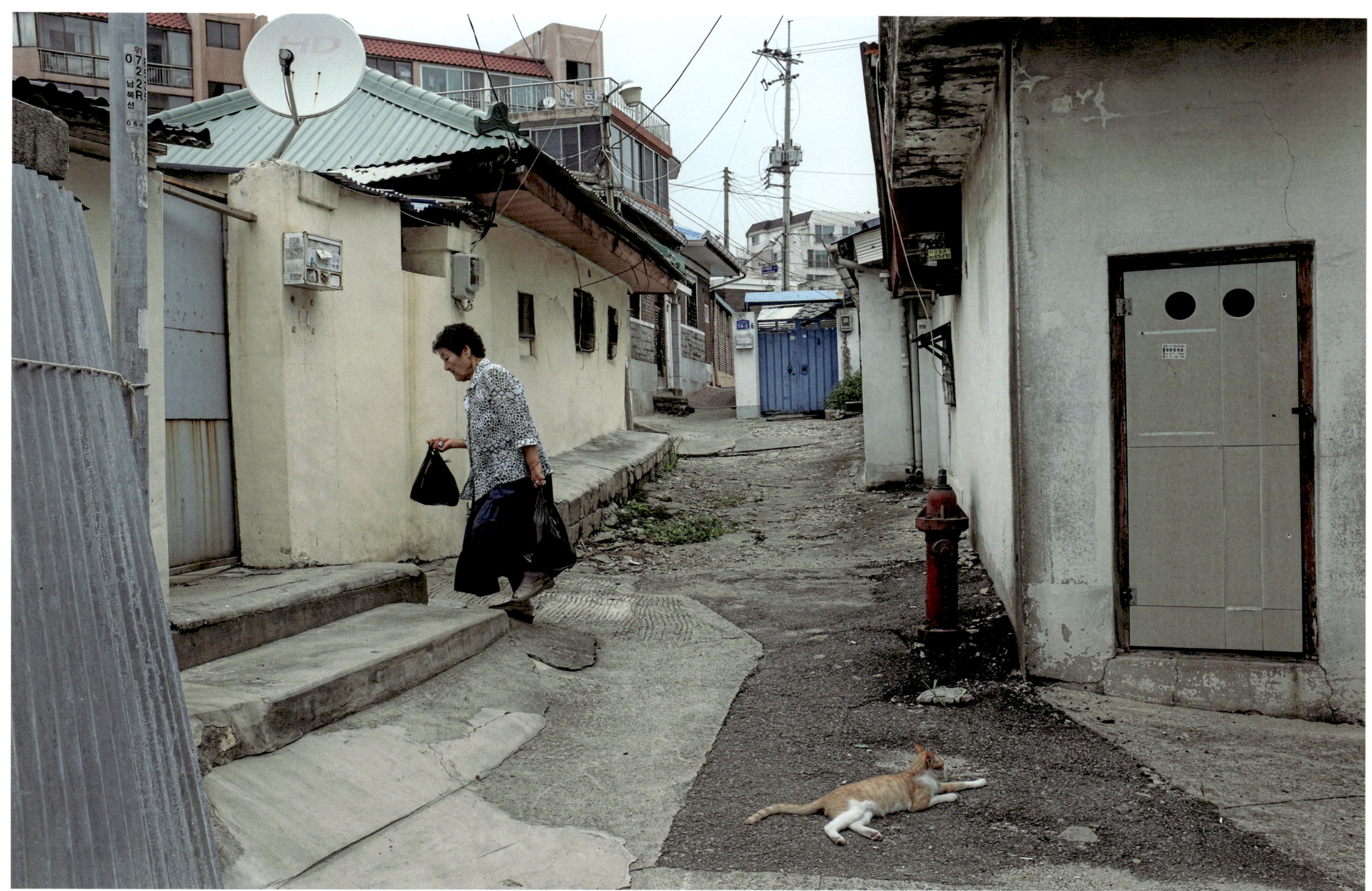

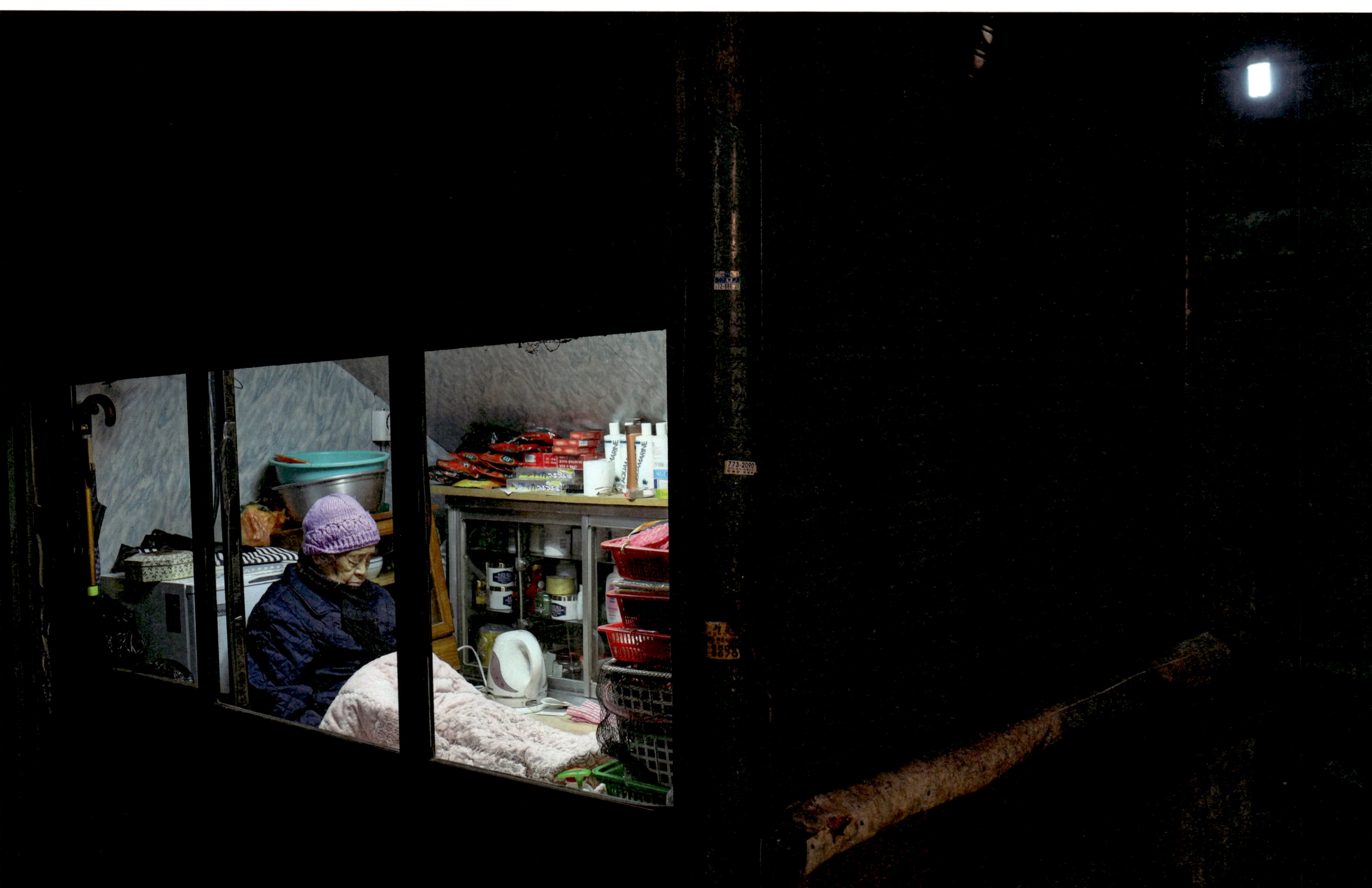

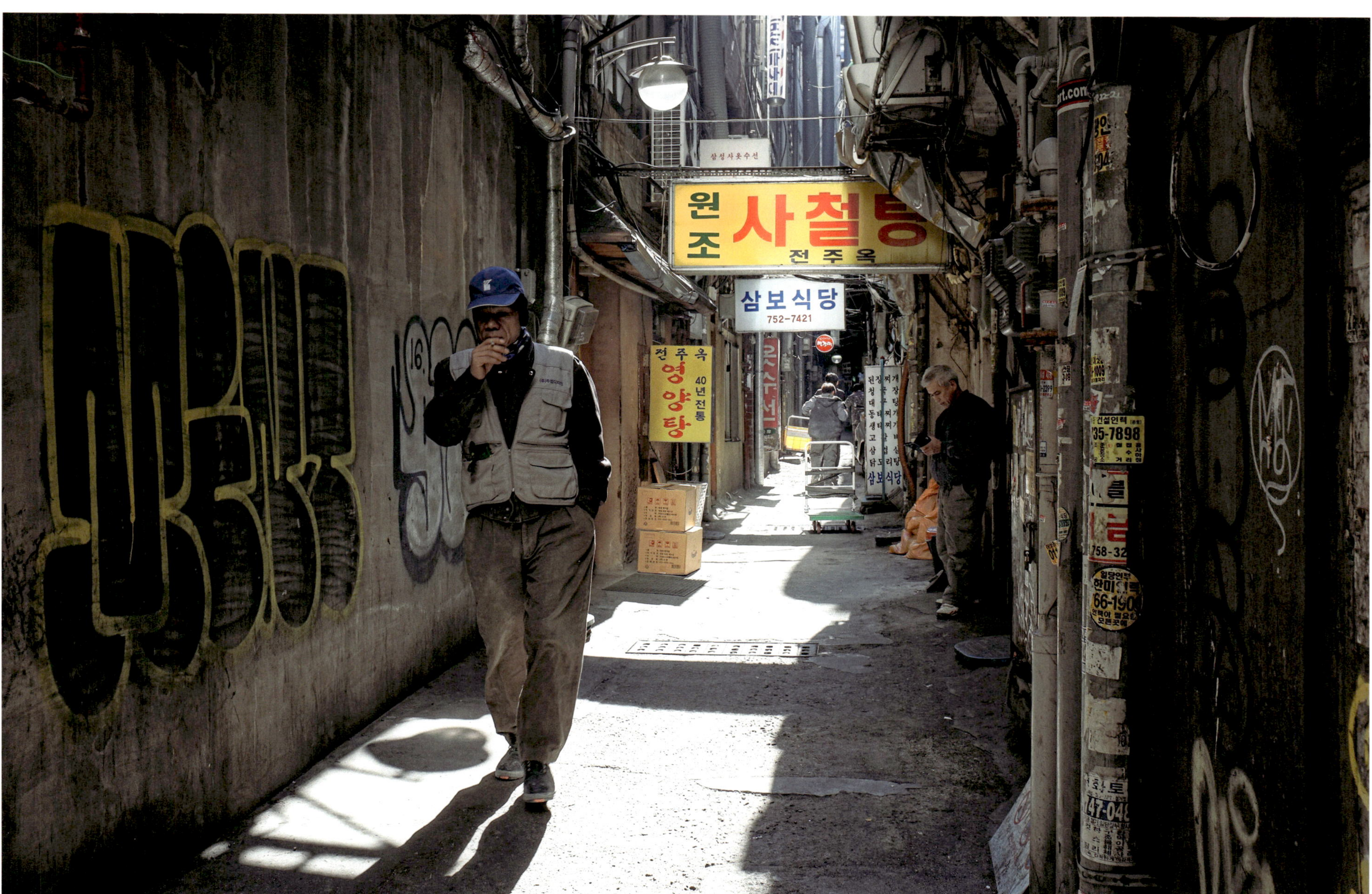
삼성사옷수선
원조 사철탕
전주옥
삼보식당
752-7421
전주옥
영양탕
40년전통
35-7898
758-32
66-190
47-048

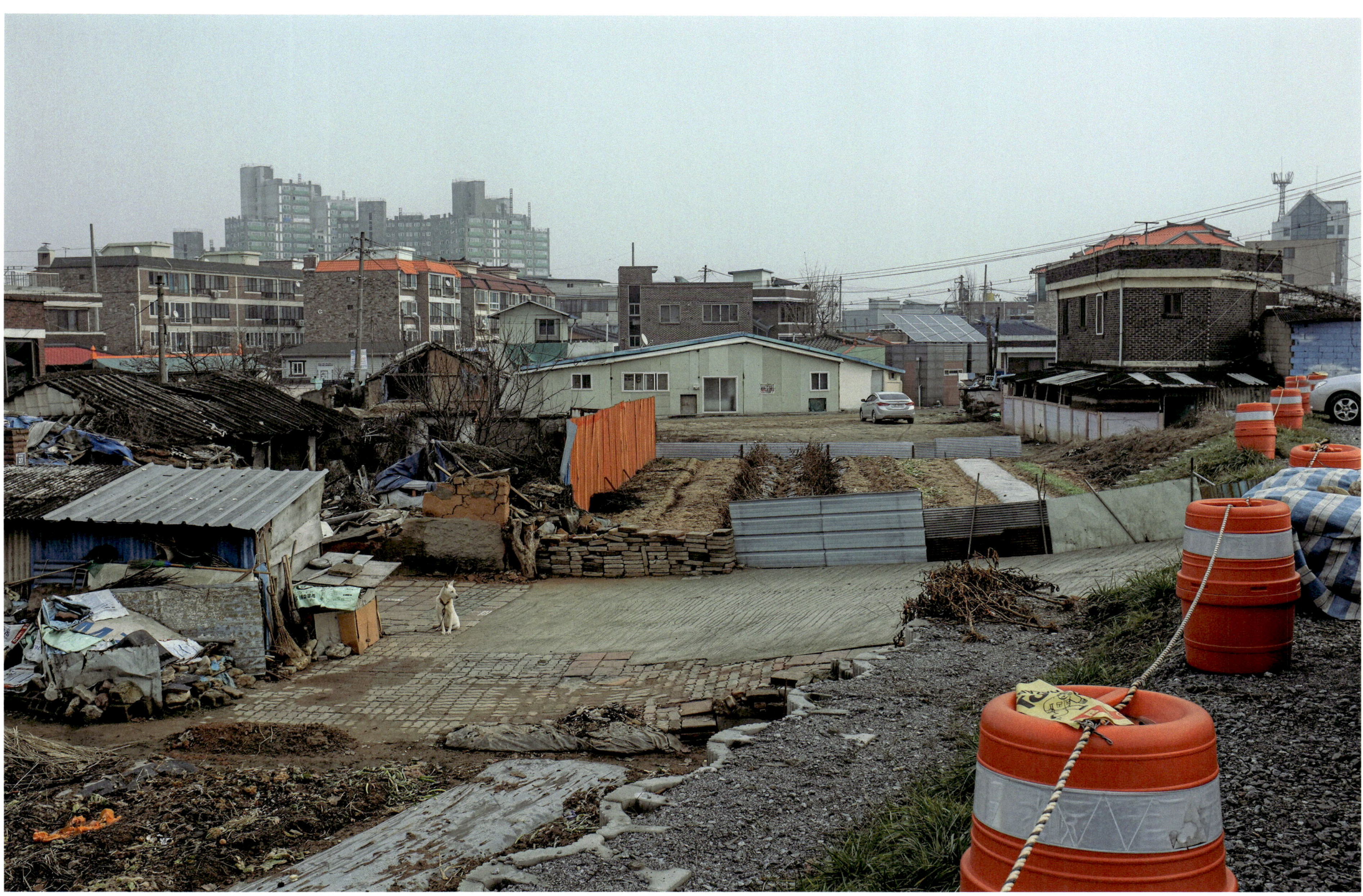

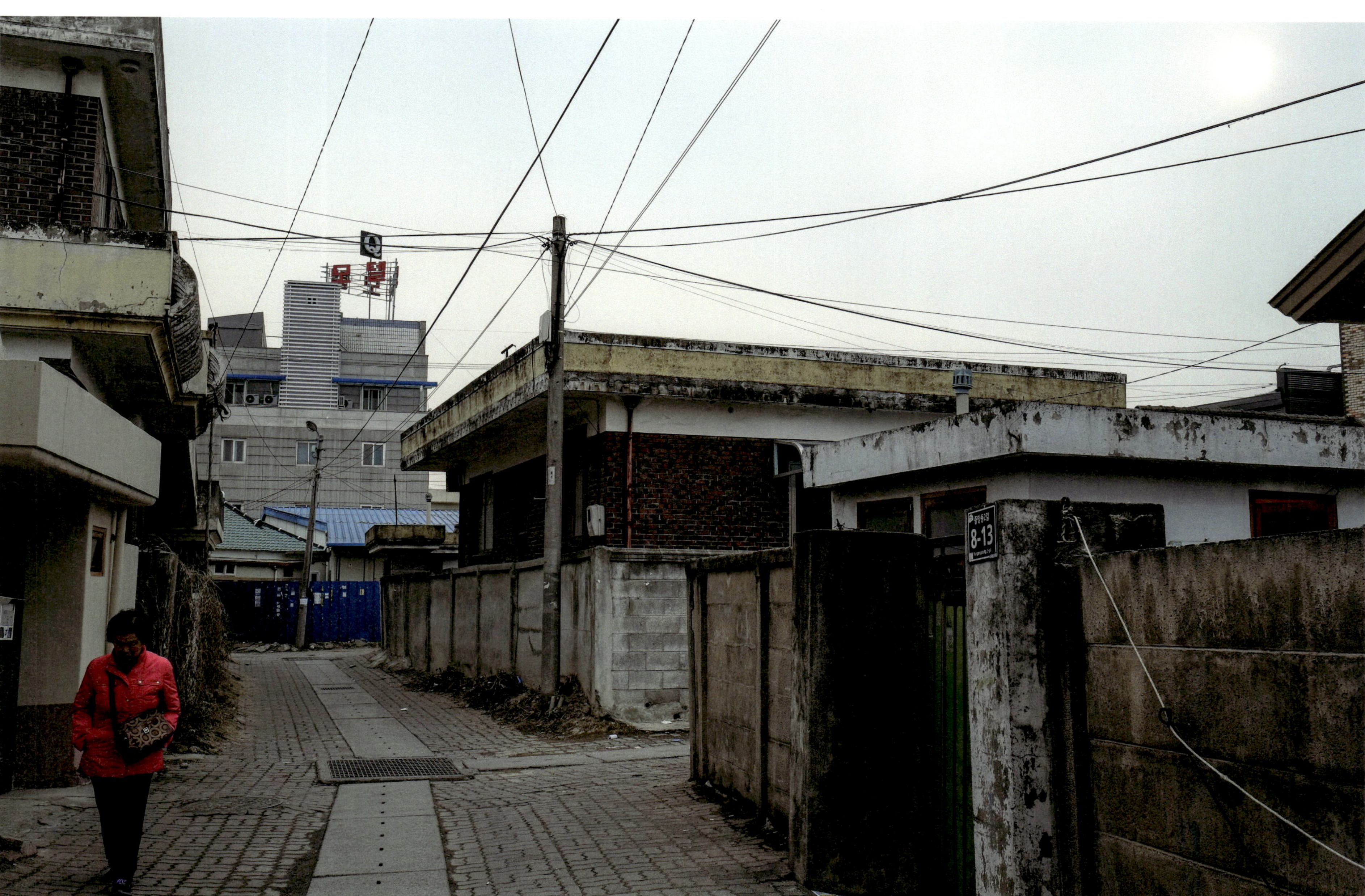

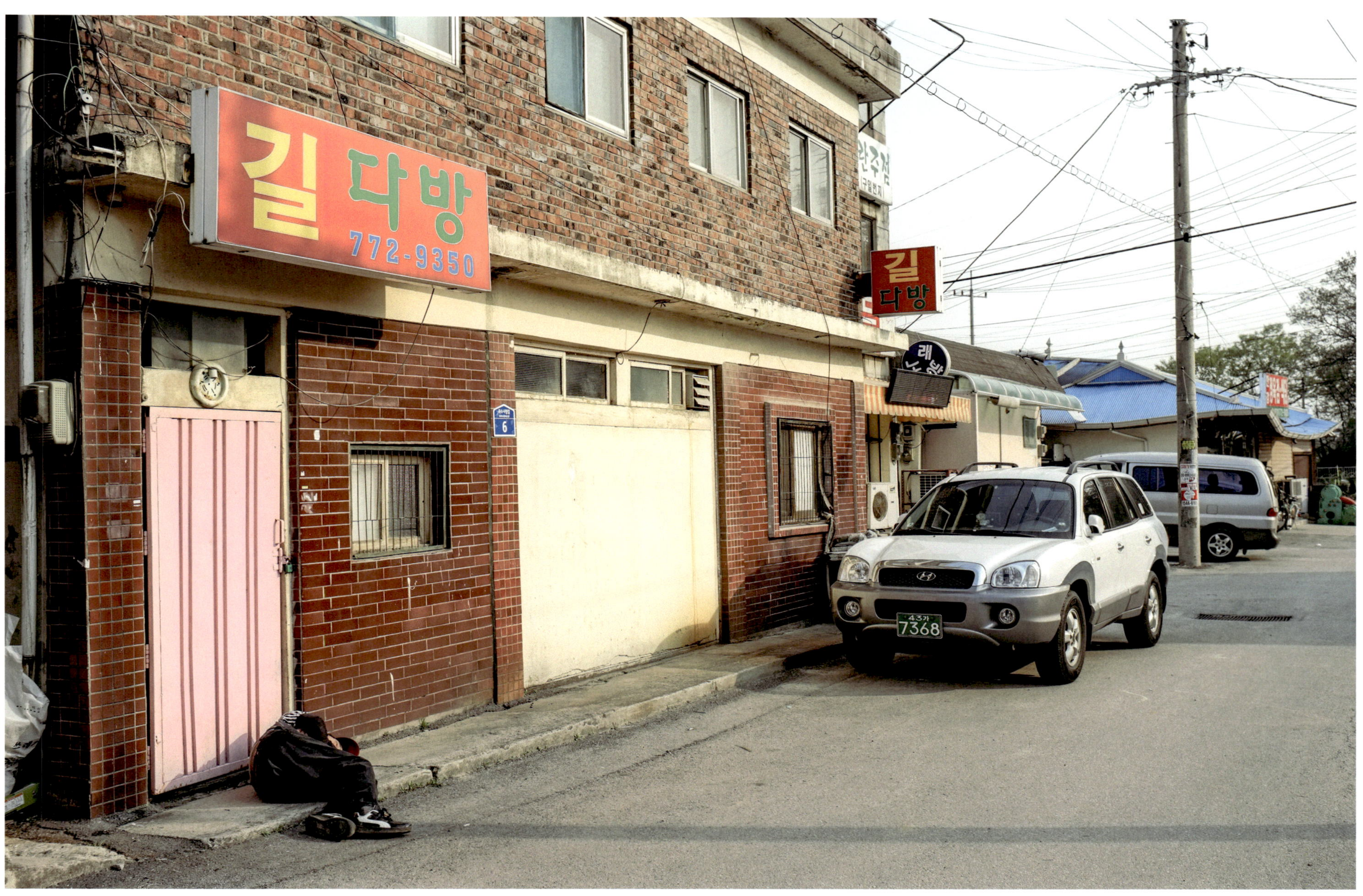
길 다방
772-9350
길
다방
6

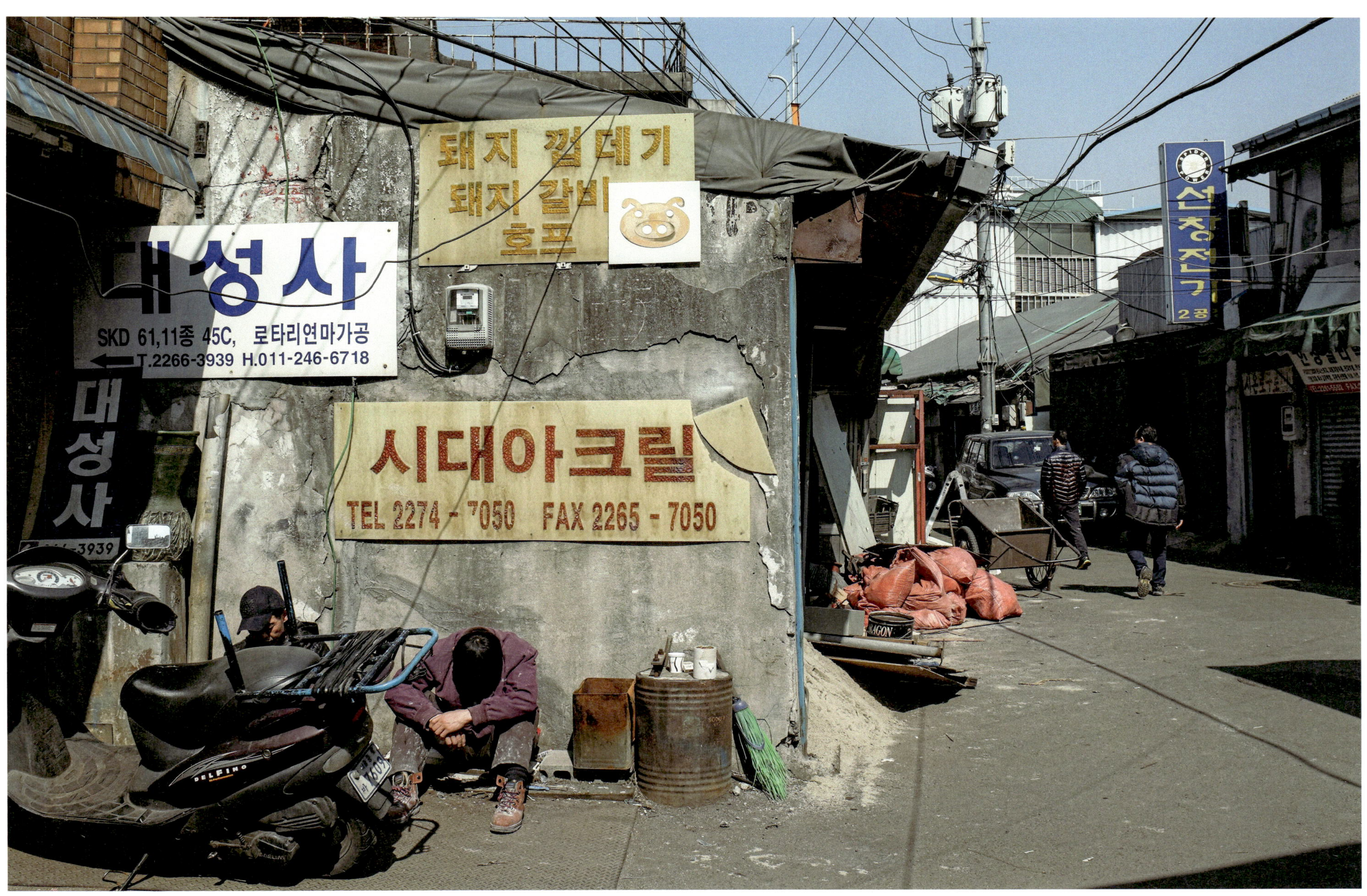
대성사
SKD 61,11종 45C, 로타리연마가공
T.2266-3939 H.011-246-6718
대성사
3939
돼지 껍데기
돼지 갈비
호프
시대아크릴
TEL 2274 - 7050   FAX 2265 - 7050
선창전기
2공
DELFINO

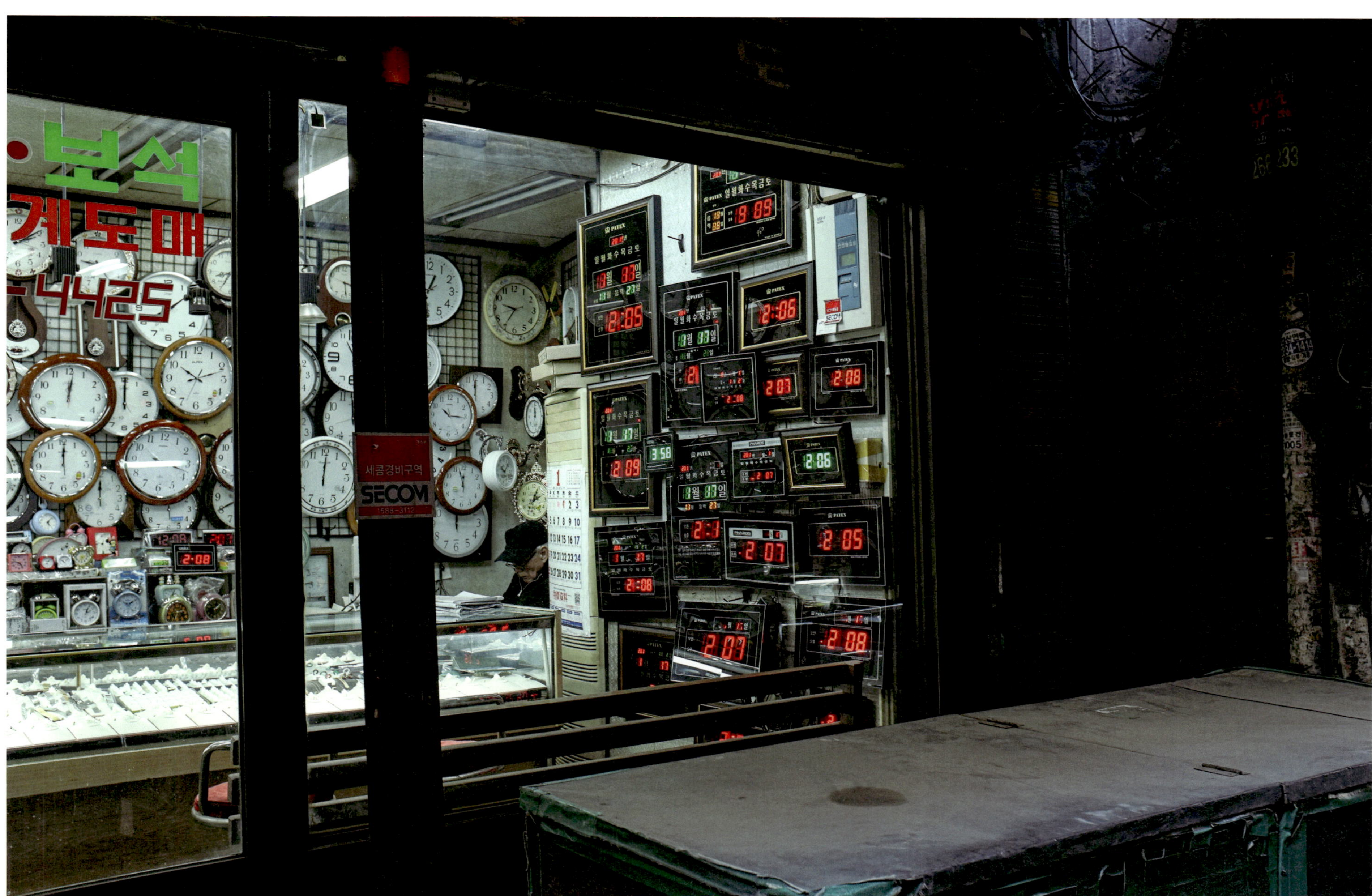
보석
시계도매
-4425
세콤경비구역
SECOM
1588-3112
PATEX
PATEX
1

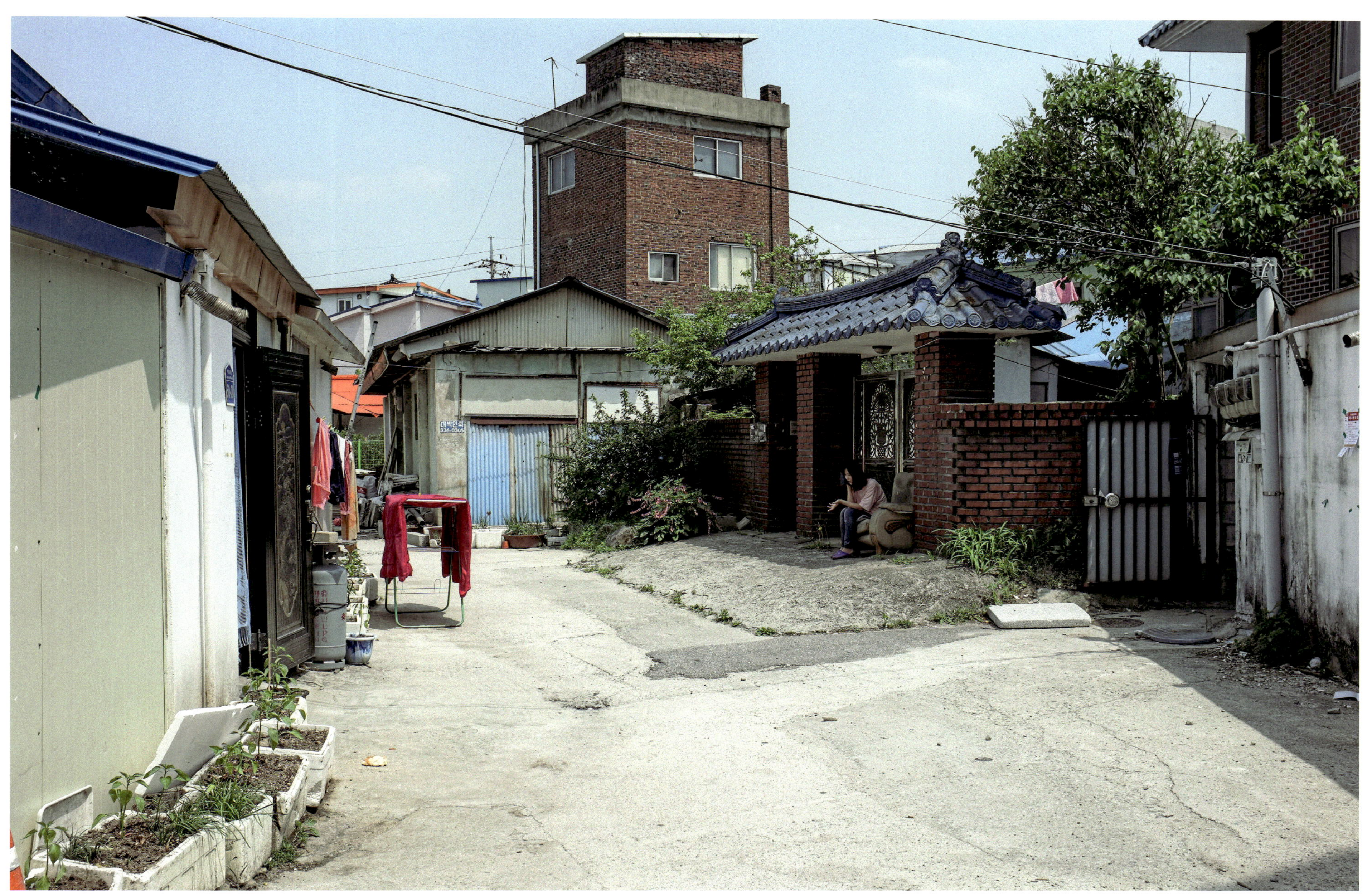

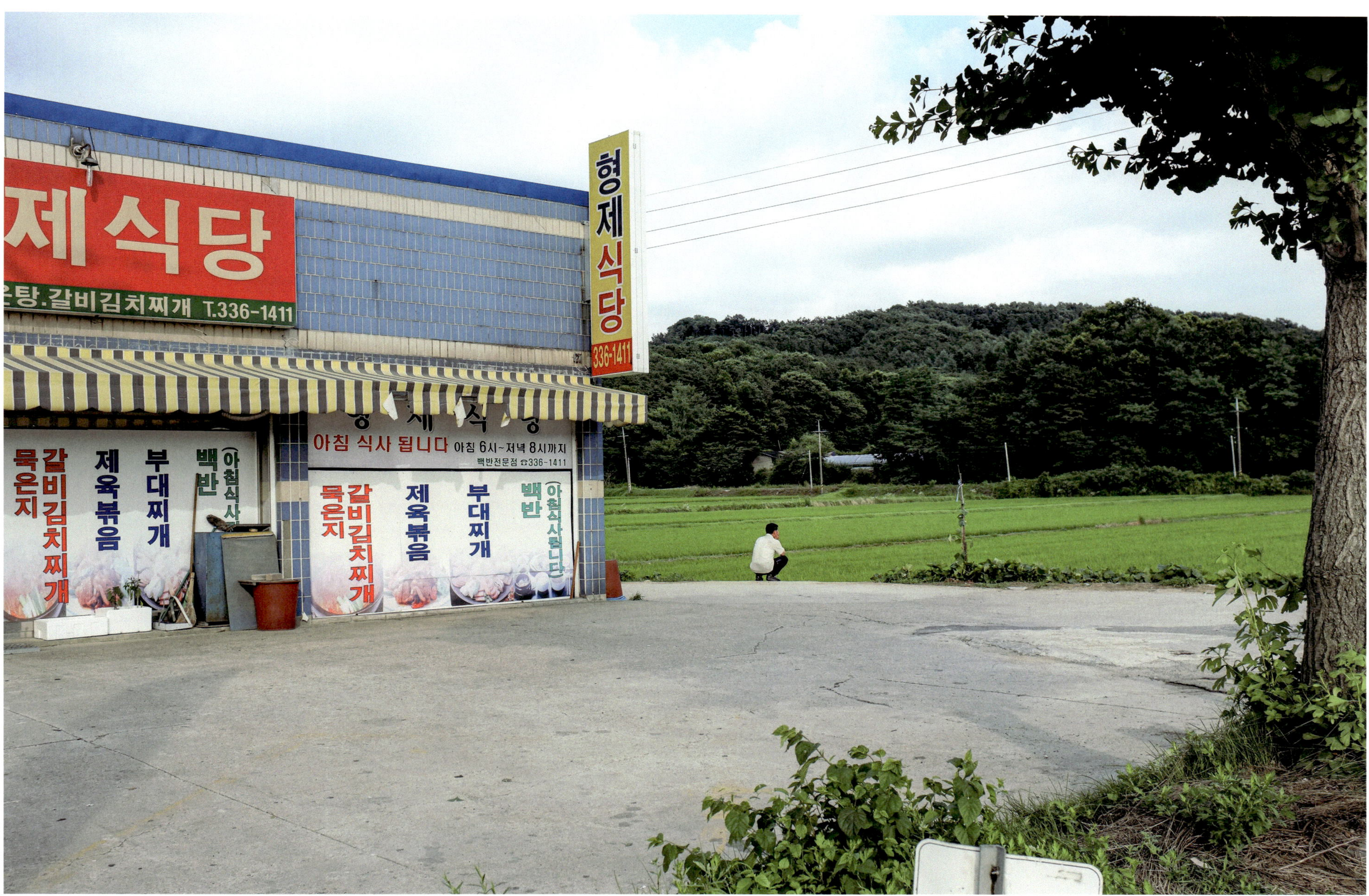
제 식당
갈비김치찌개 T.336-1411
형제식당
336-1411
형제식당
아침 식사 됩니다 아침 6시~저녁 8시까지
백반전문점 ☎336-1411
묵은지
갈비김치찌개
제육볶음
부대찌개
백반
아침식사됩니다

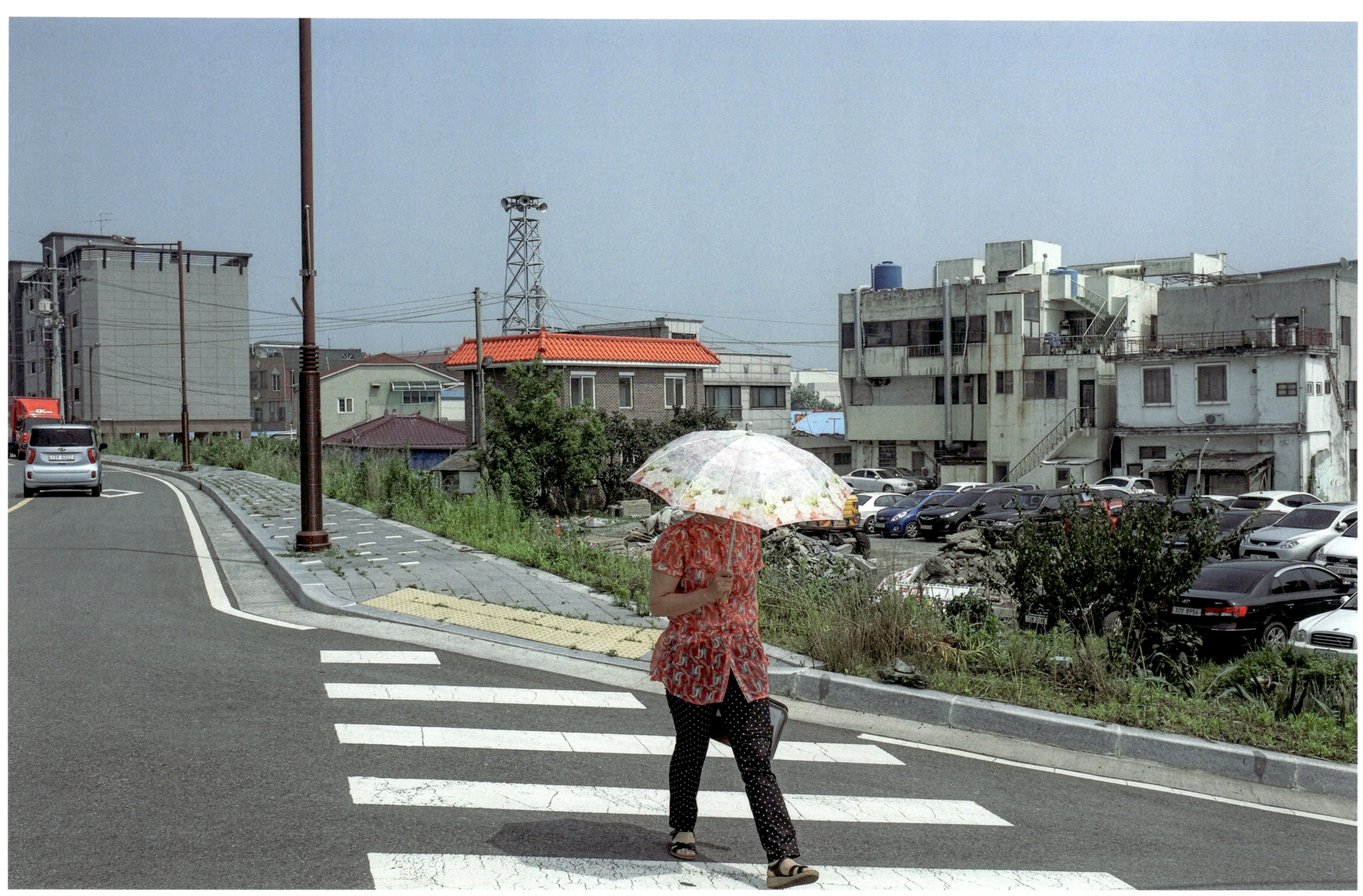

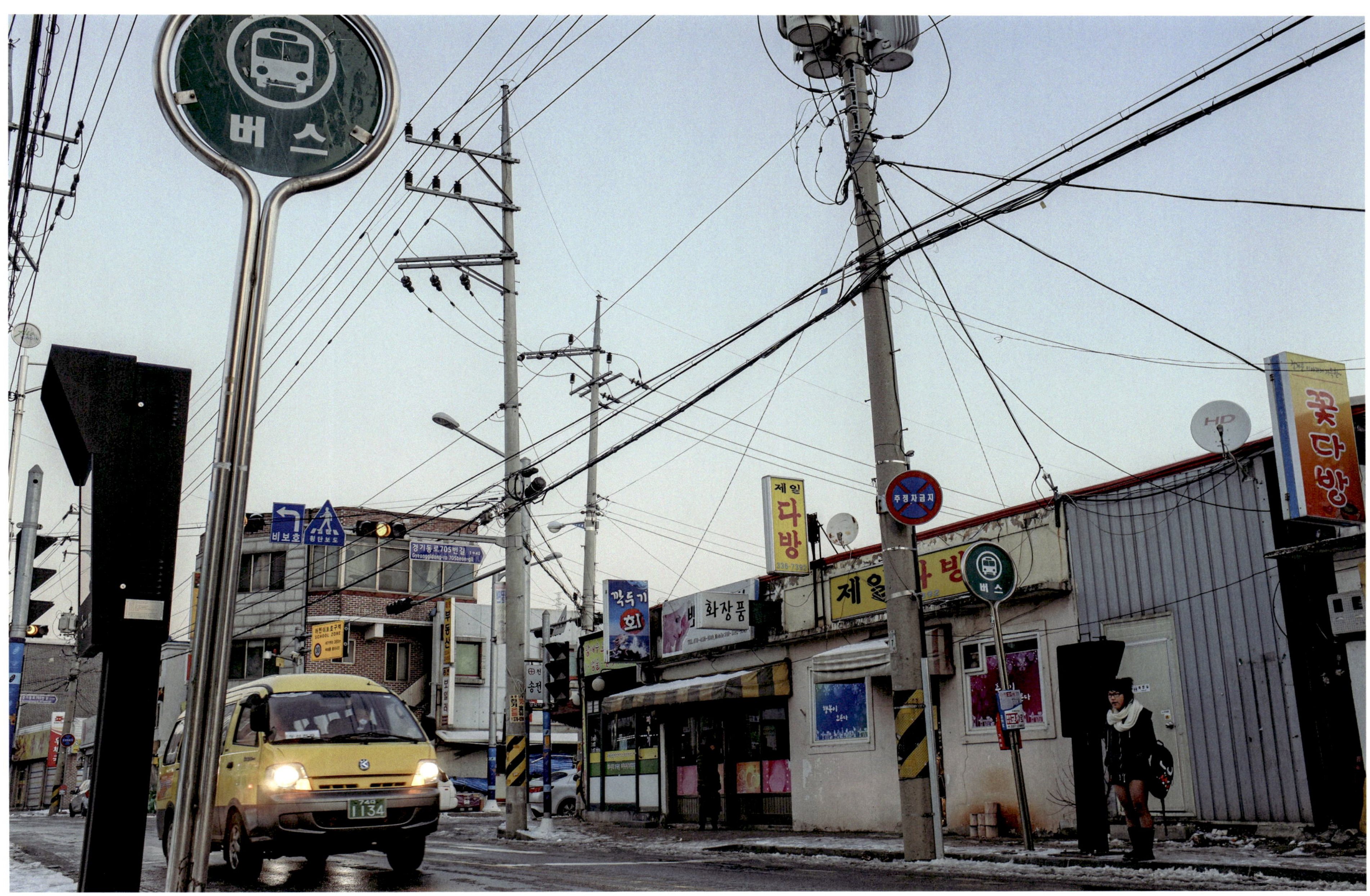
버스
제일
다방
제일 다방
깍득기
회
화장품
꽃다방
비보호
횡단보도
경기동로705번길
Gyeonggidong-ro 705beon-gil
주정차금지
버스
HD
SCHOOL ZONE
1134

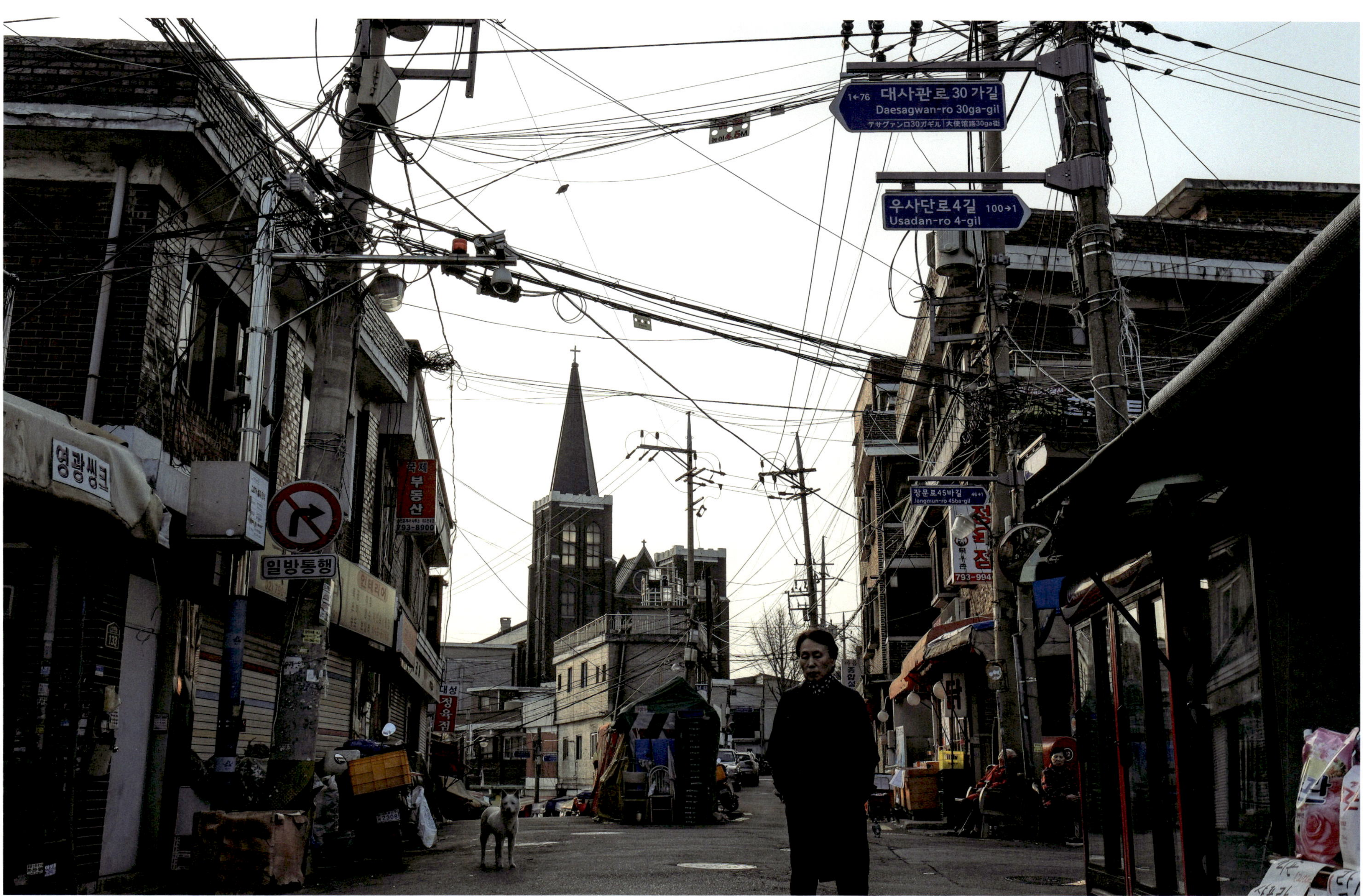

대사관로30가길
1←76
Daesagwan-ro 30ga-gil
テサグァンロ30ガギル｜大使館路30ga街
우사단로4길
100→1
Usadan-ro 4-gil
장문로45바길
46→1
Jangmun-ro 45ba-gil
영광씽크
국제
부동산
793-8900
대성
정육점
일방통행
인테리어
정
육
점
793-994

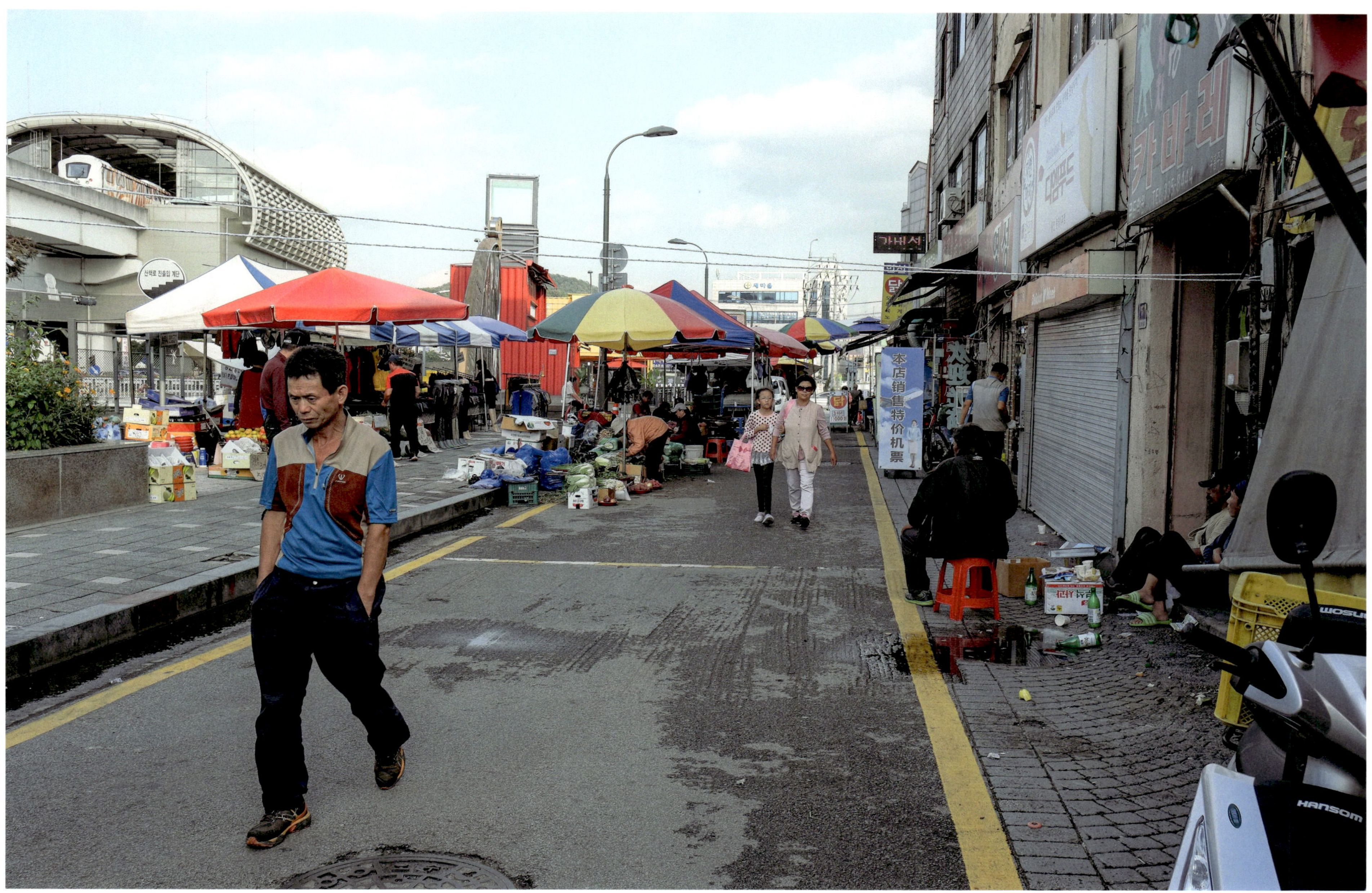

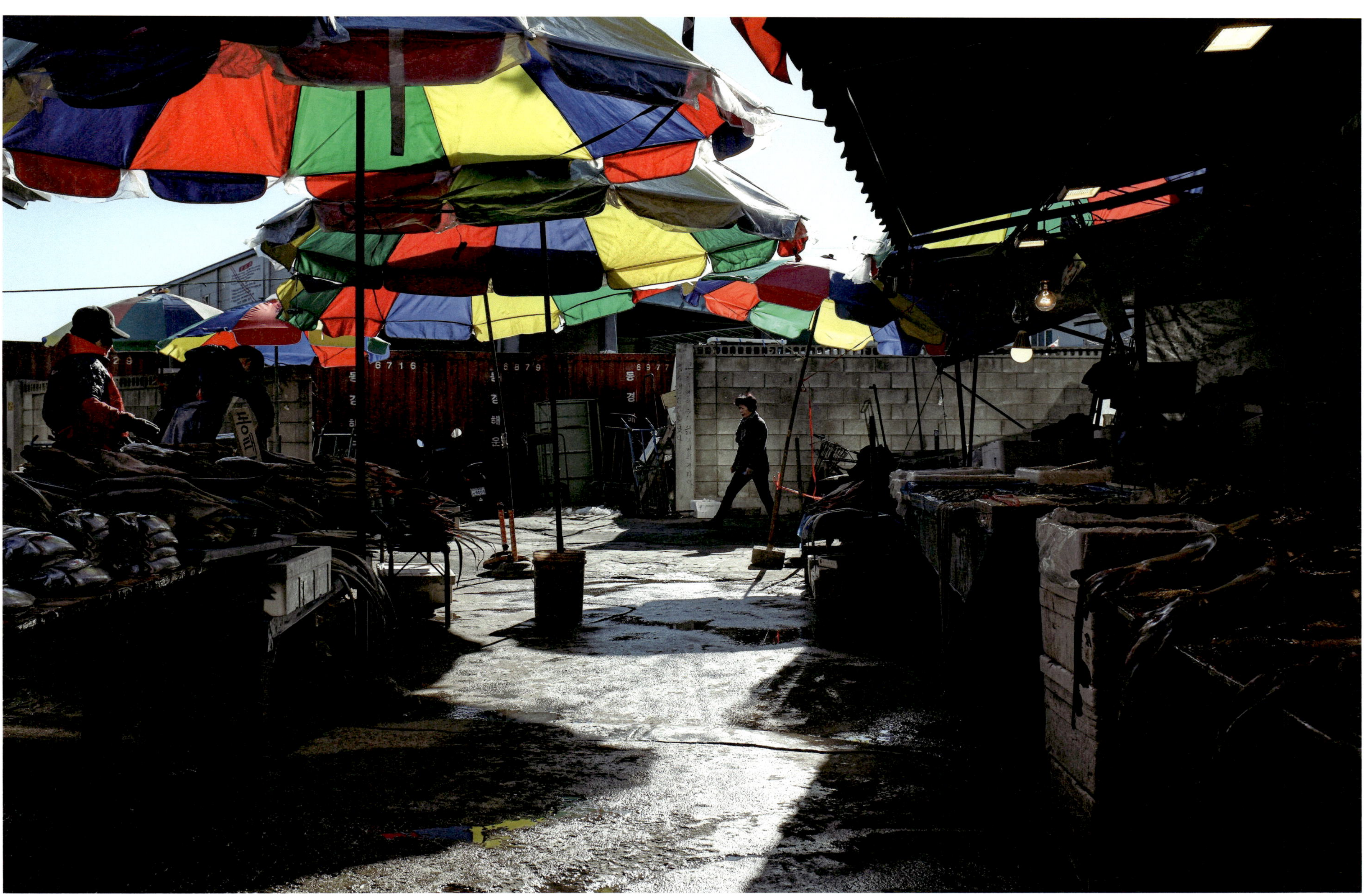

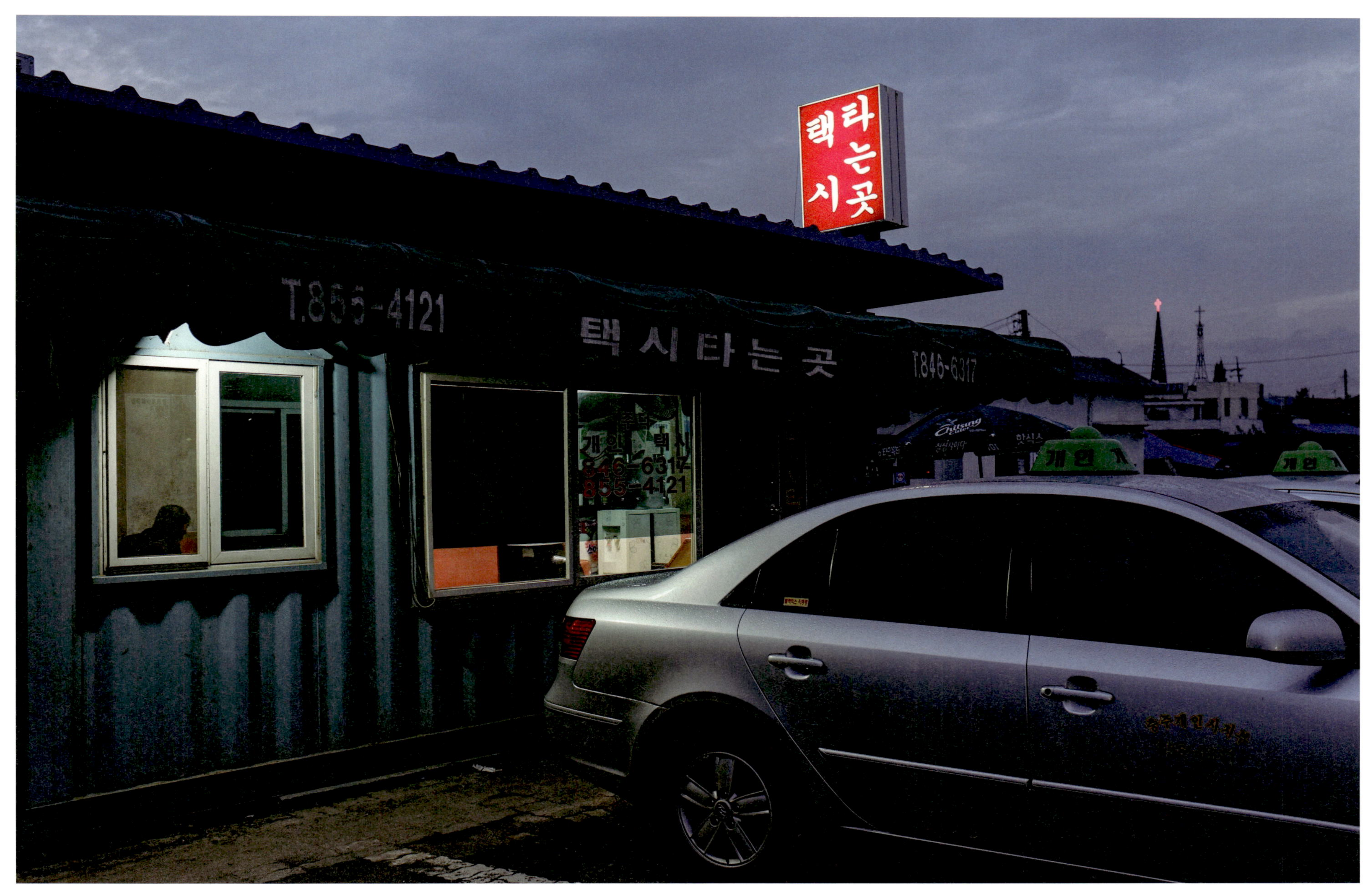
택 타
시 는
  곳
T.855-4121
택시타는곳
T.846-6317
개인 택시
846-6317
855-4121
개인
개인

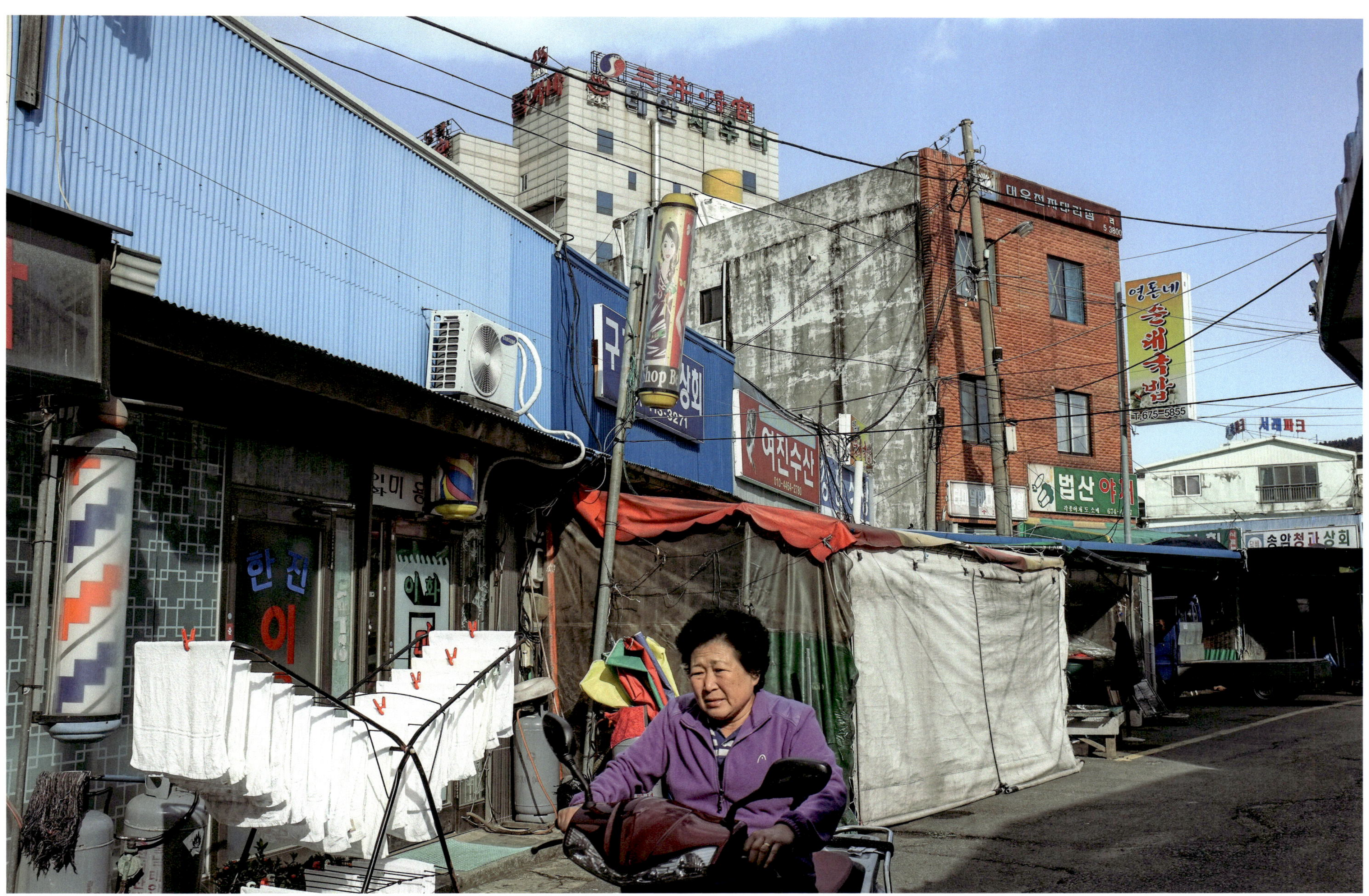
구안 각수당
대우전짜단리찜
5 3800
영돈네
술애국밥
675-5855
구
hop B상회
115-3271
여진수산
010-4464-2700
법산 야지
세레파크
송악청과상회
한진
이화

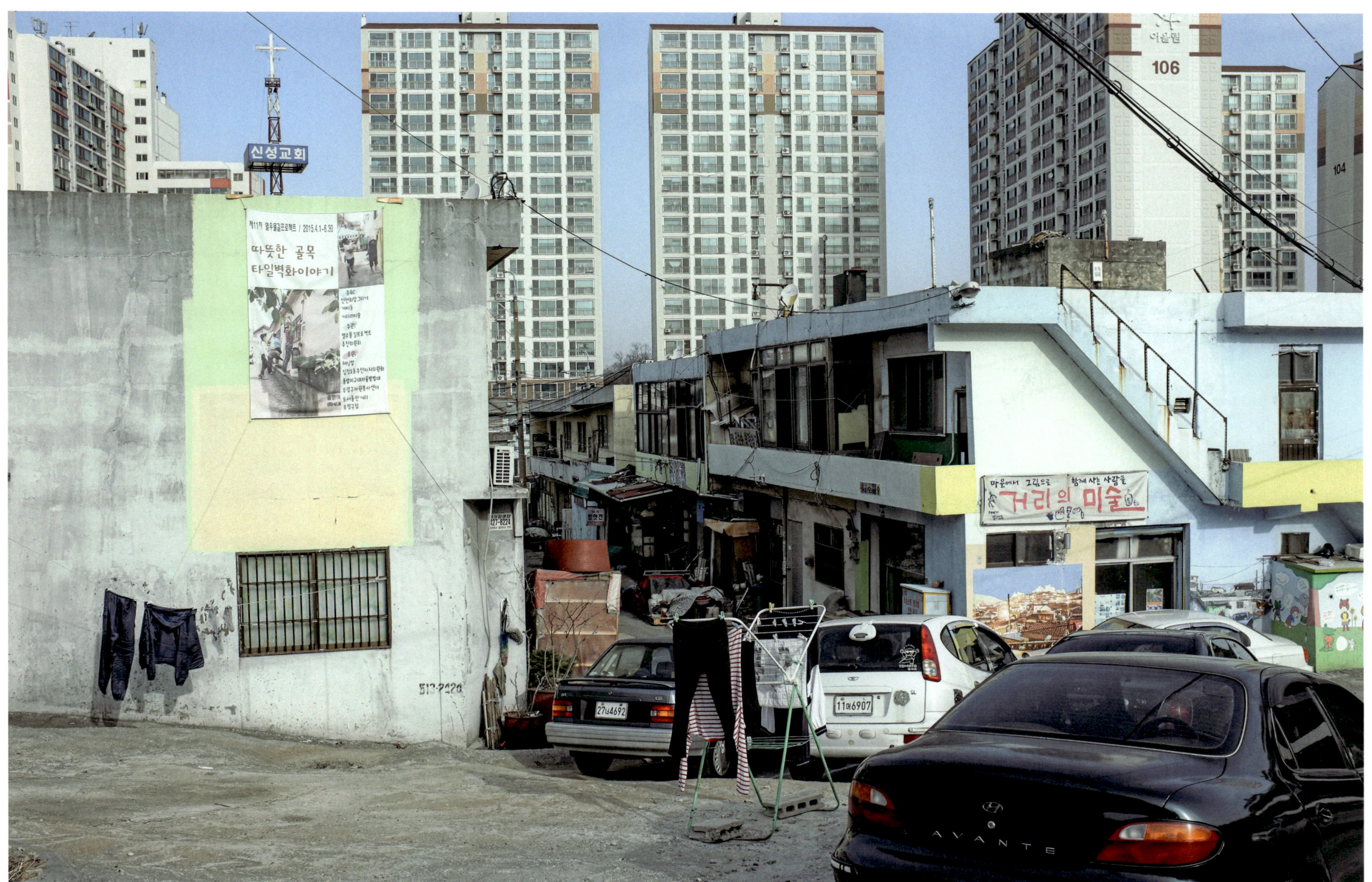

신성교회
106
104
제11기 달우물골프로젝트 / 2015.4.1~6.30
따뜻한 골목
타일벽화이야기
마음에서 그림으로 함께 사는 사람들
거리의 미술
AVANTE

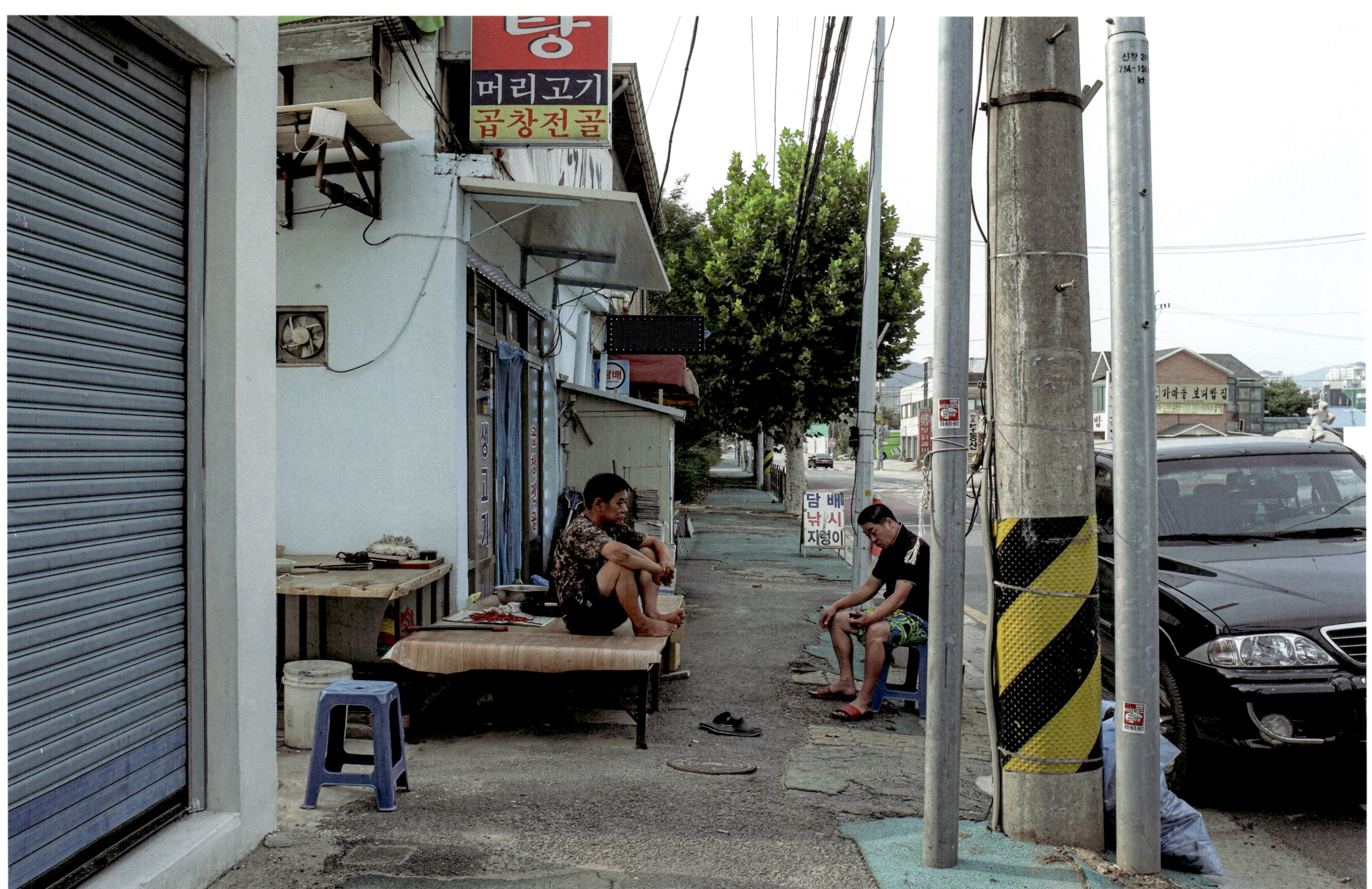
탕
머리고기
곱창전골
생고기
곱창전골
담배
낚시
지렁이
가마솥 보리밥집

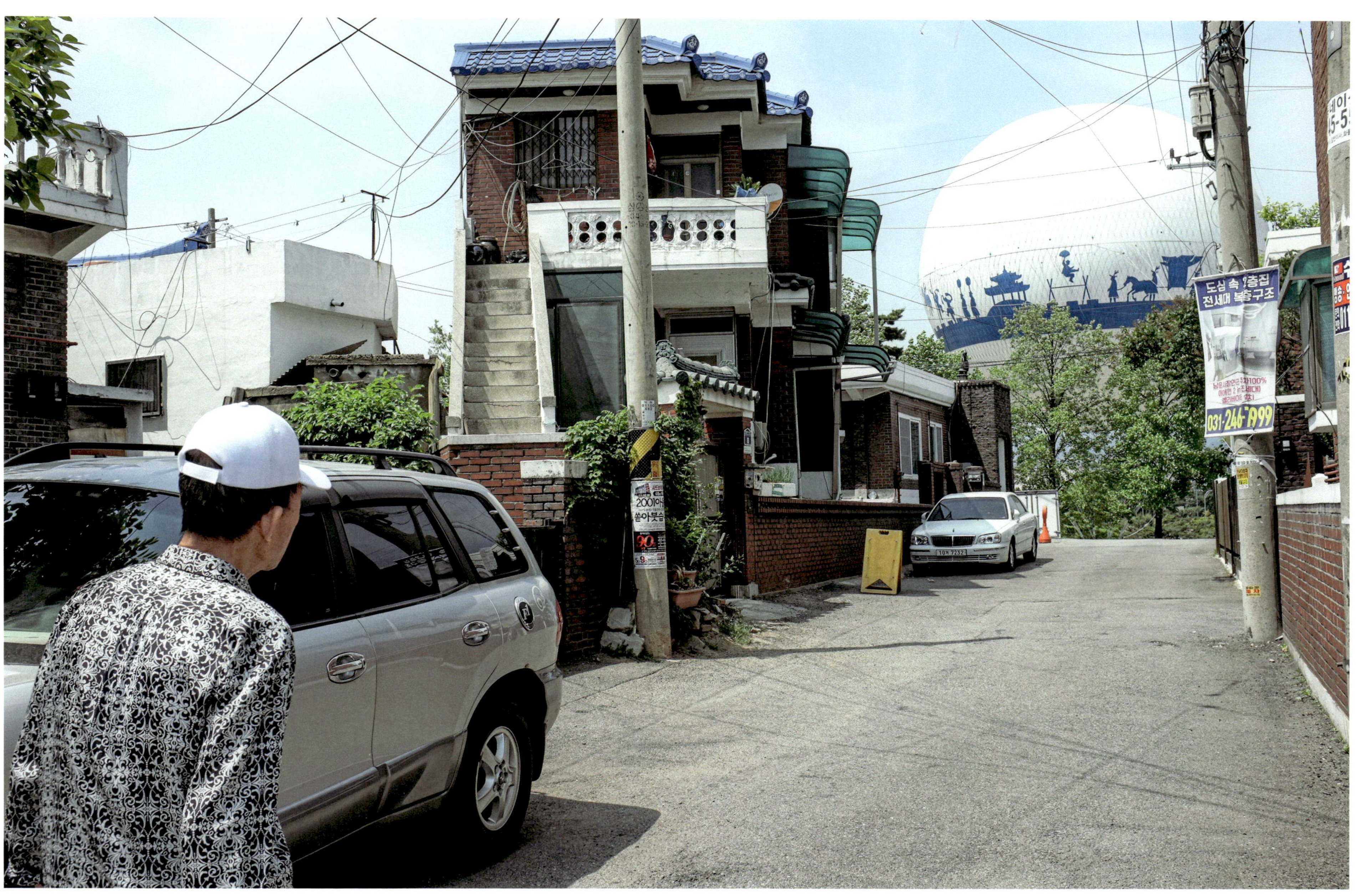
도심 속 1층집
전세내 복층구조
031-246-A99

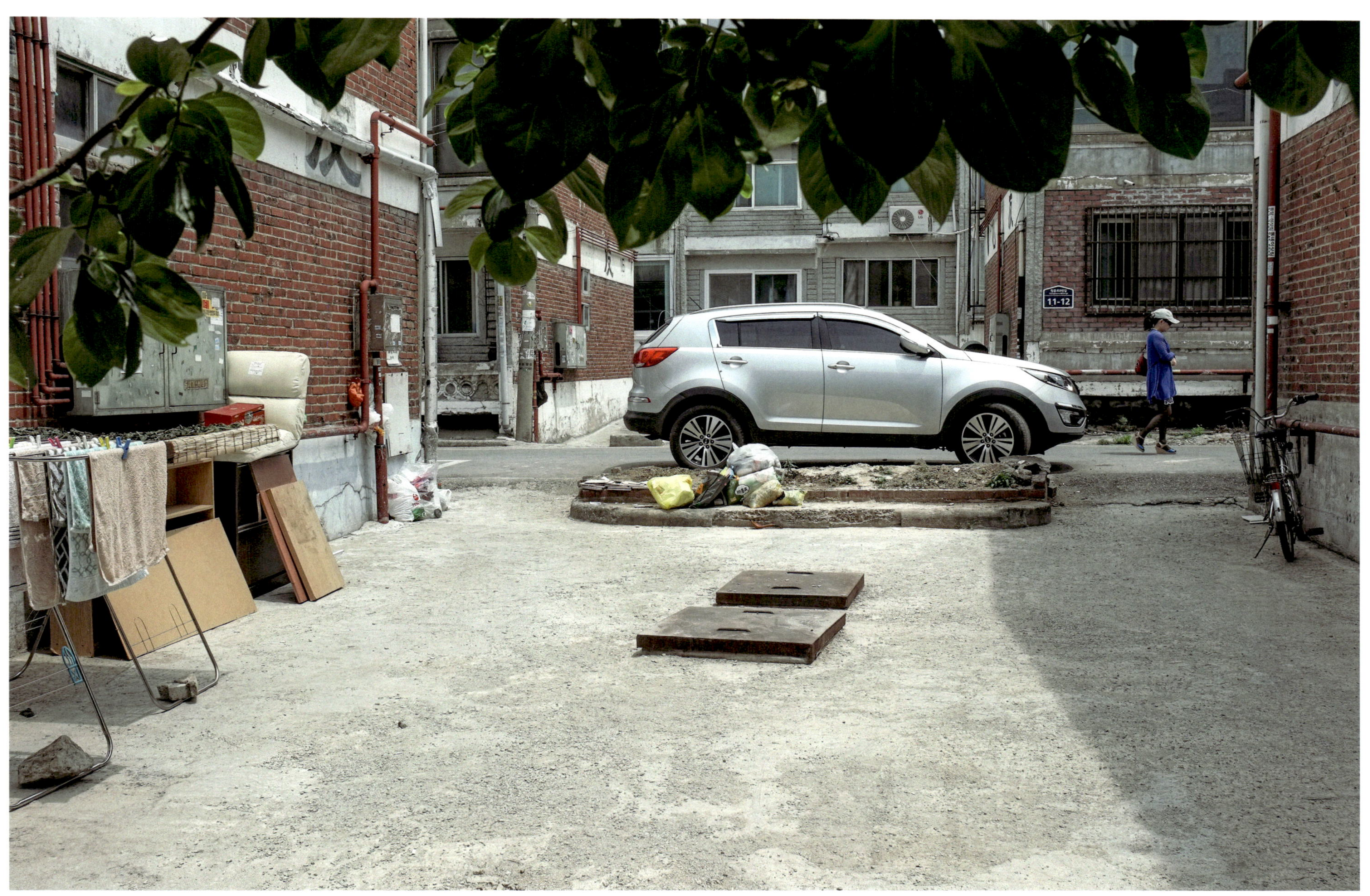

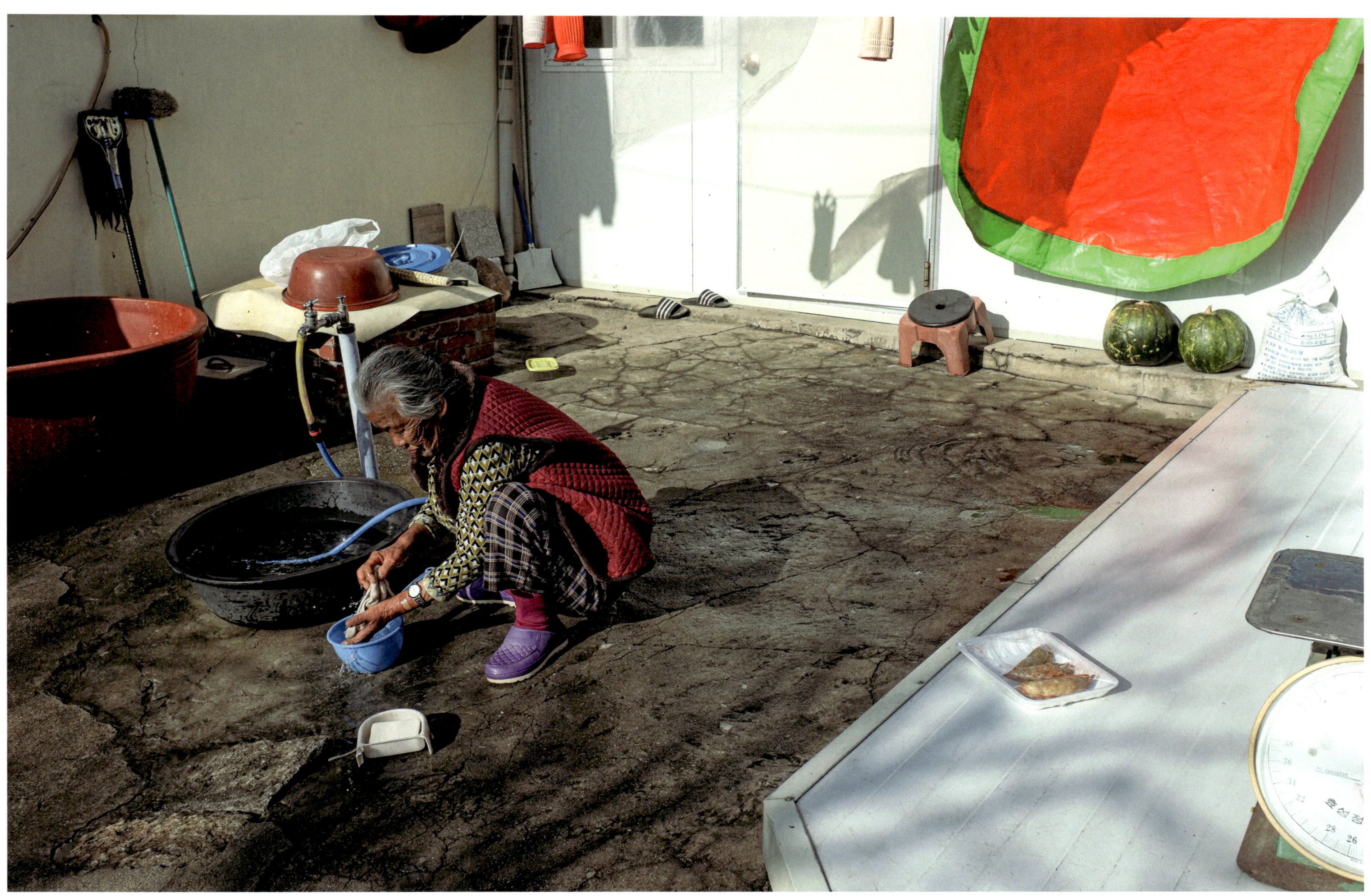

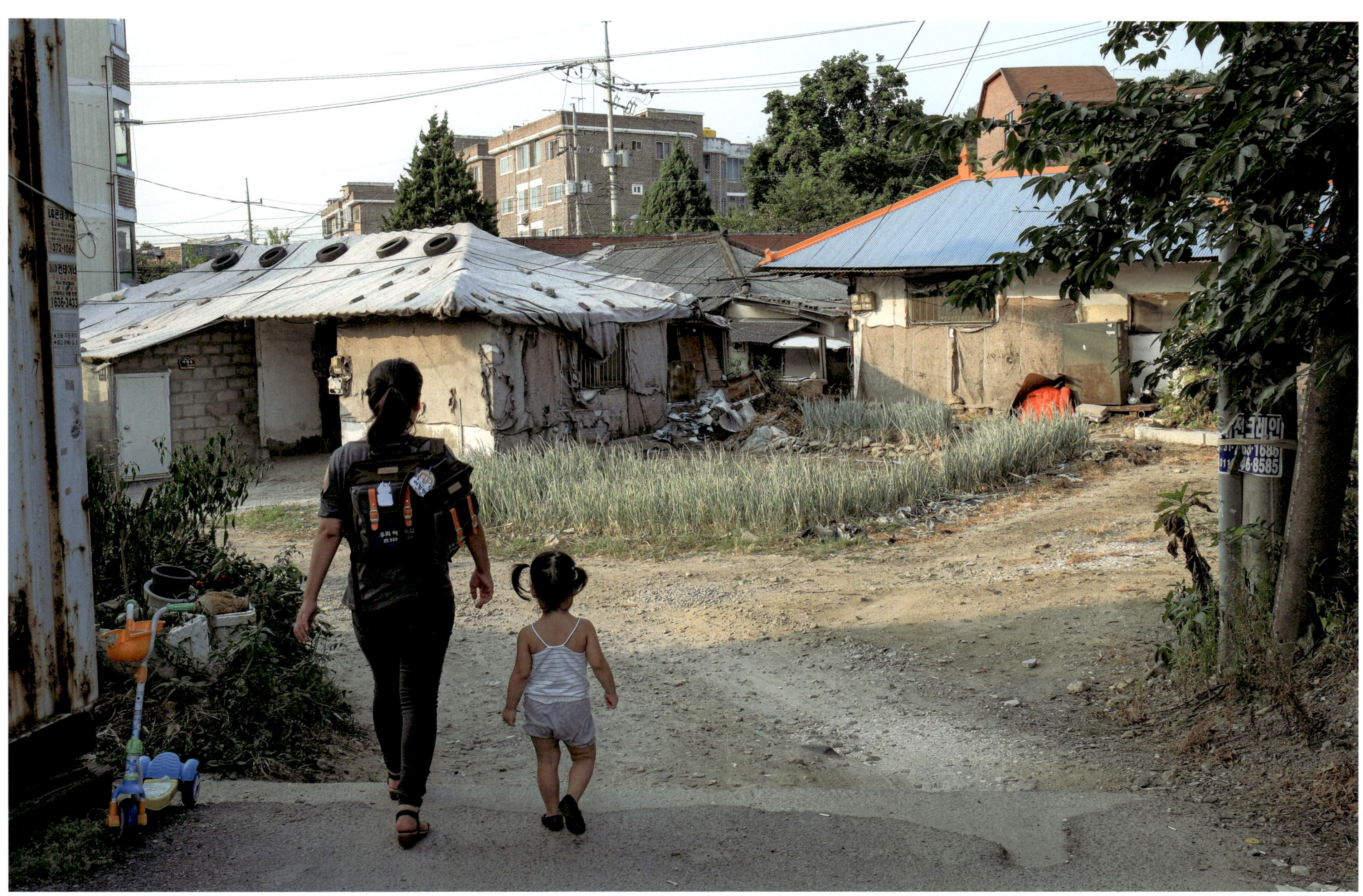

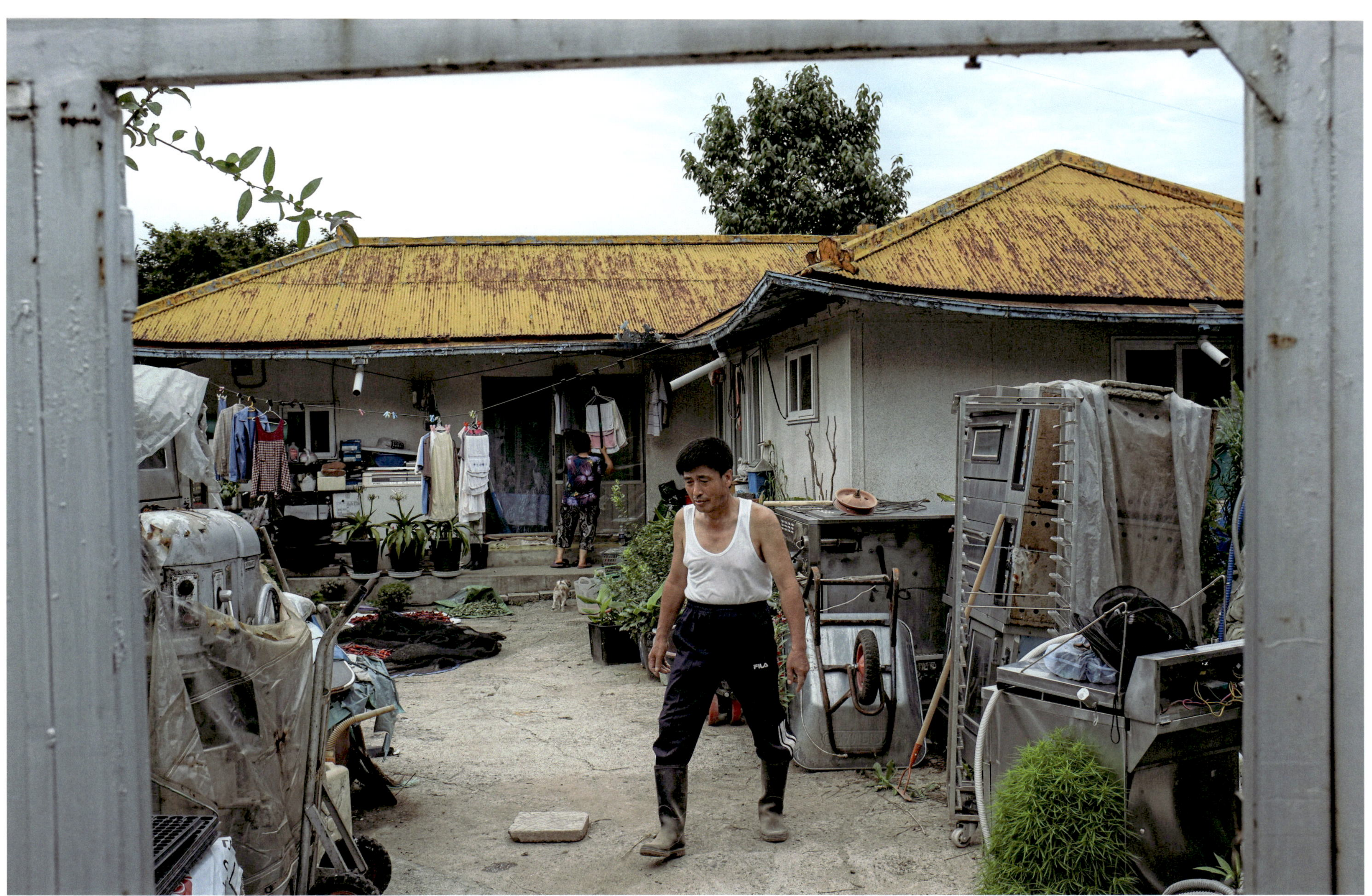

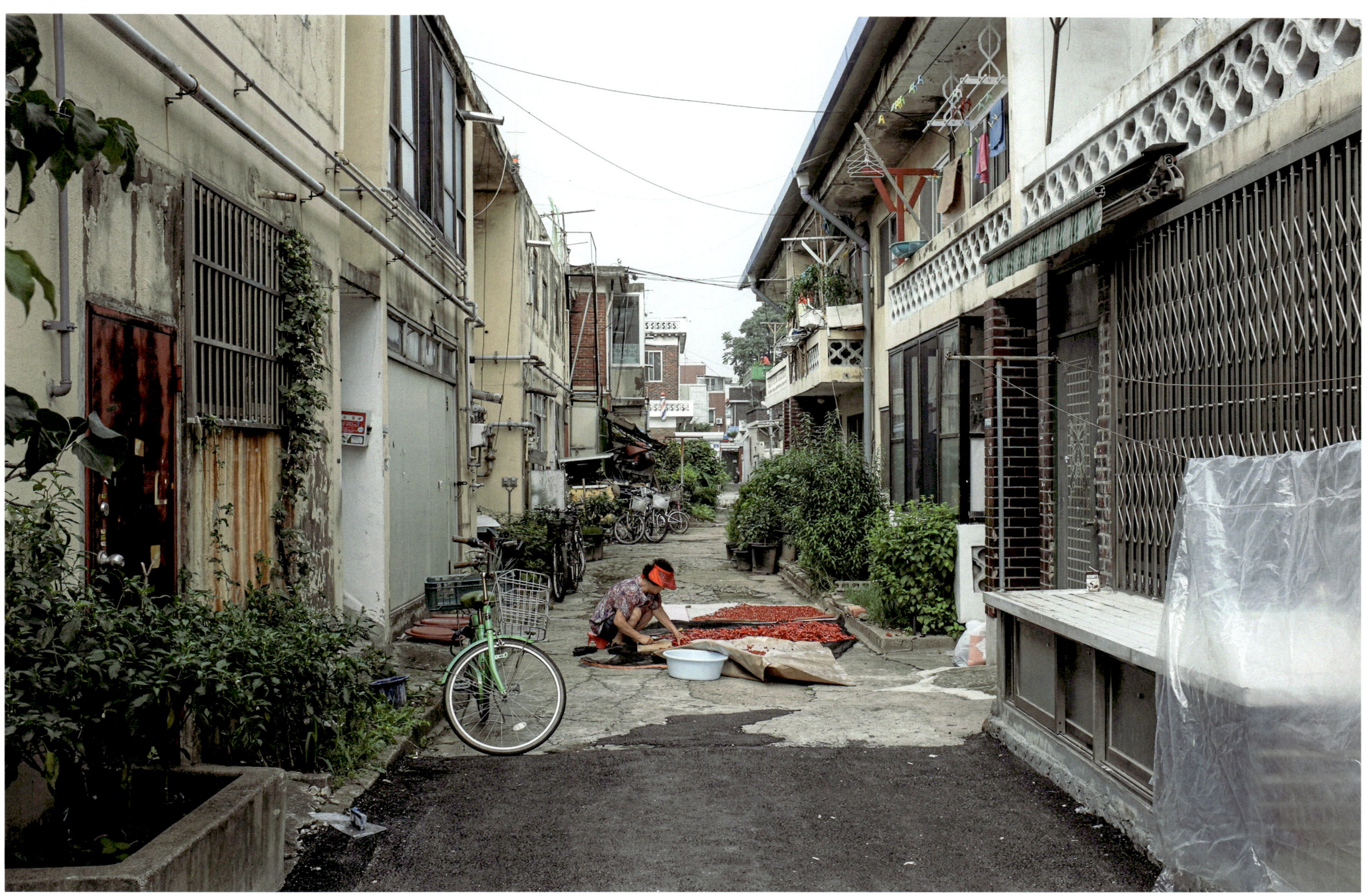

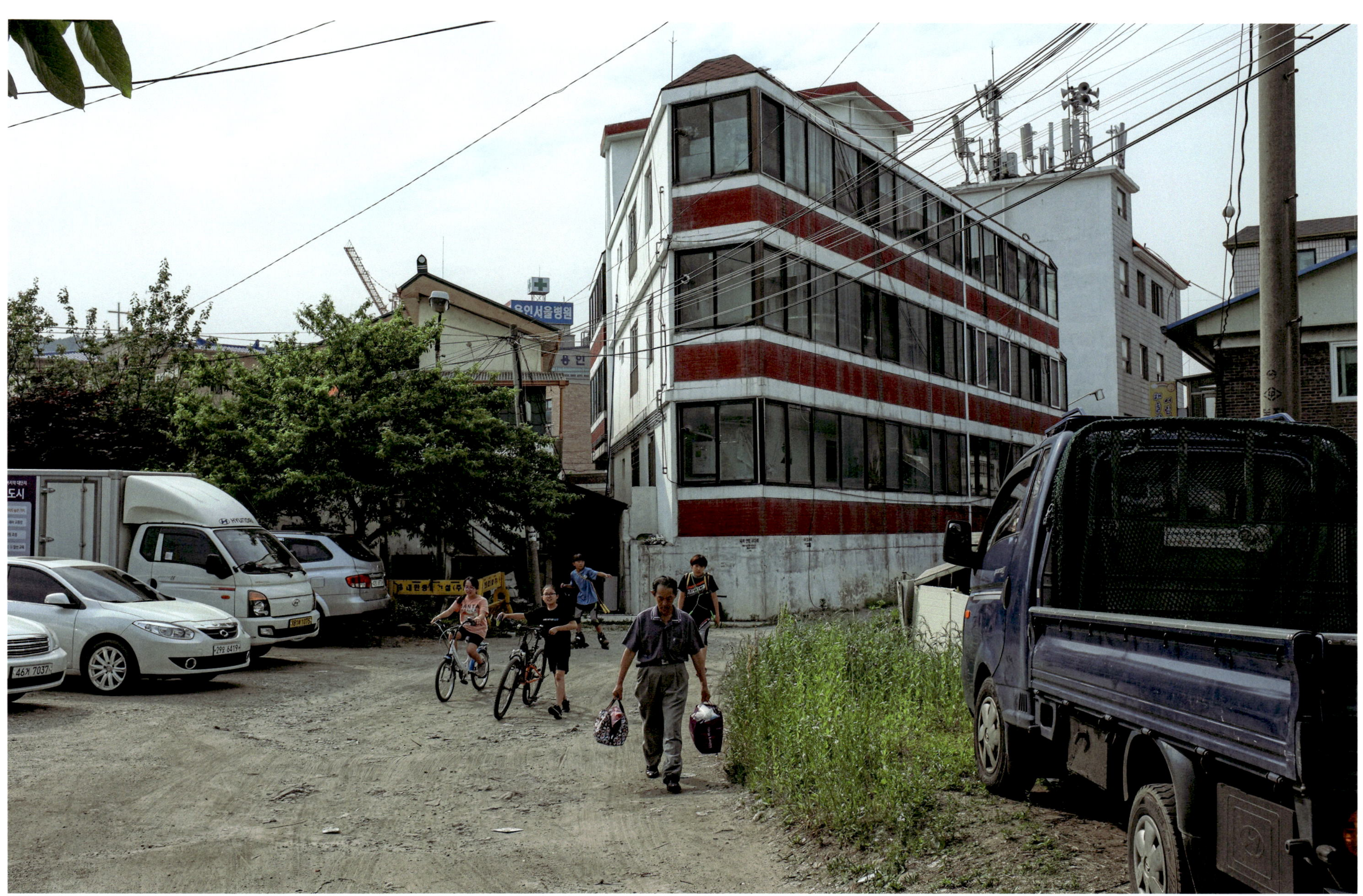

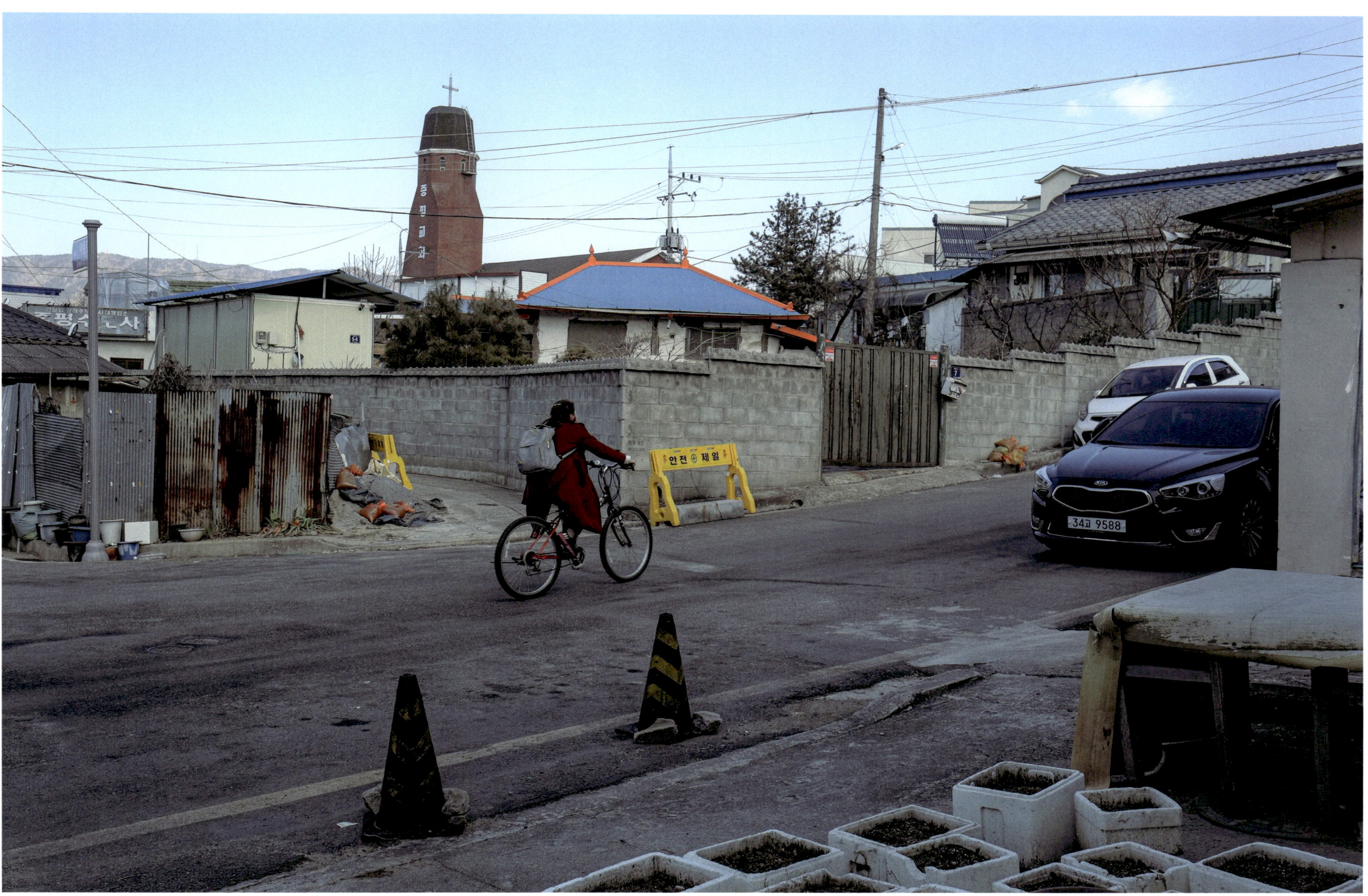

중앙교회
안전 제일
34고 9588

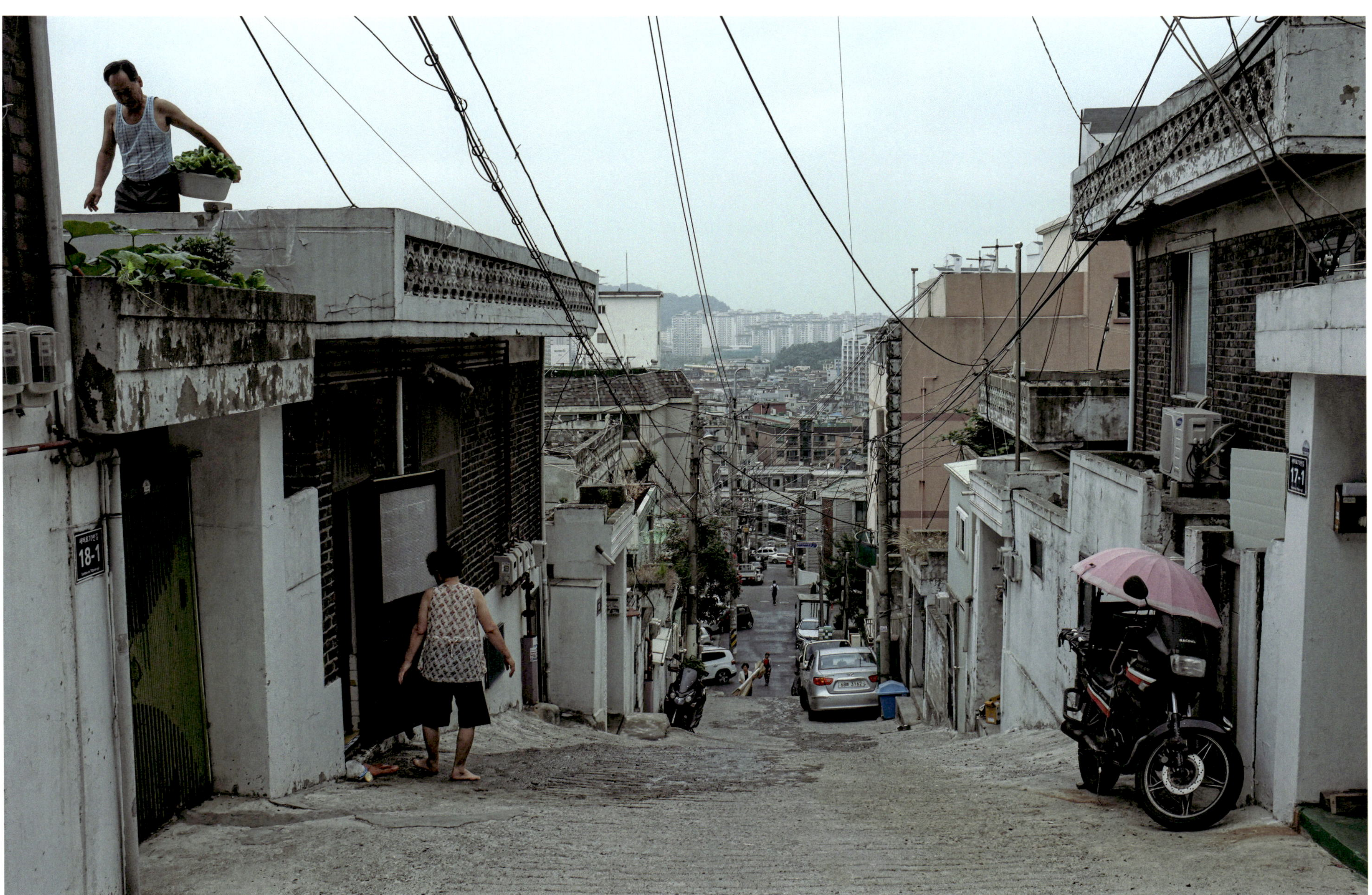

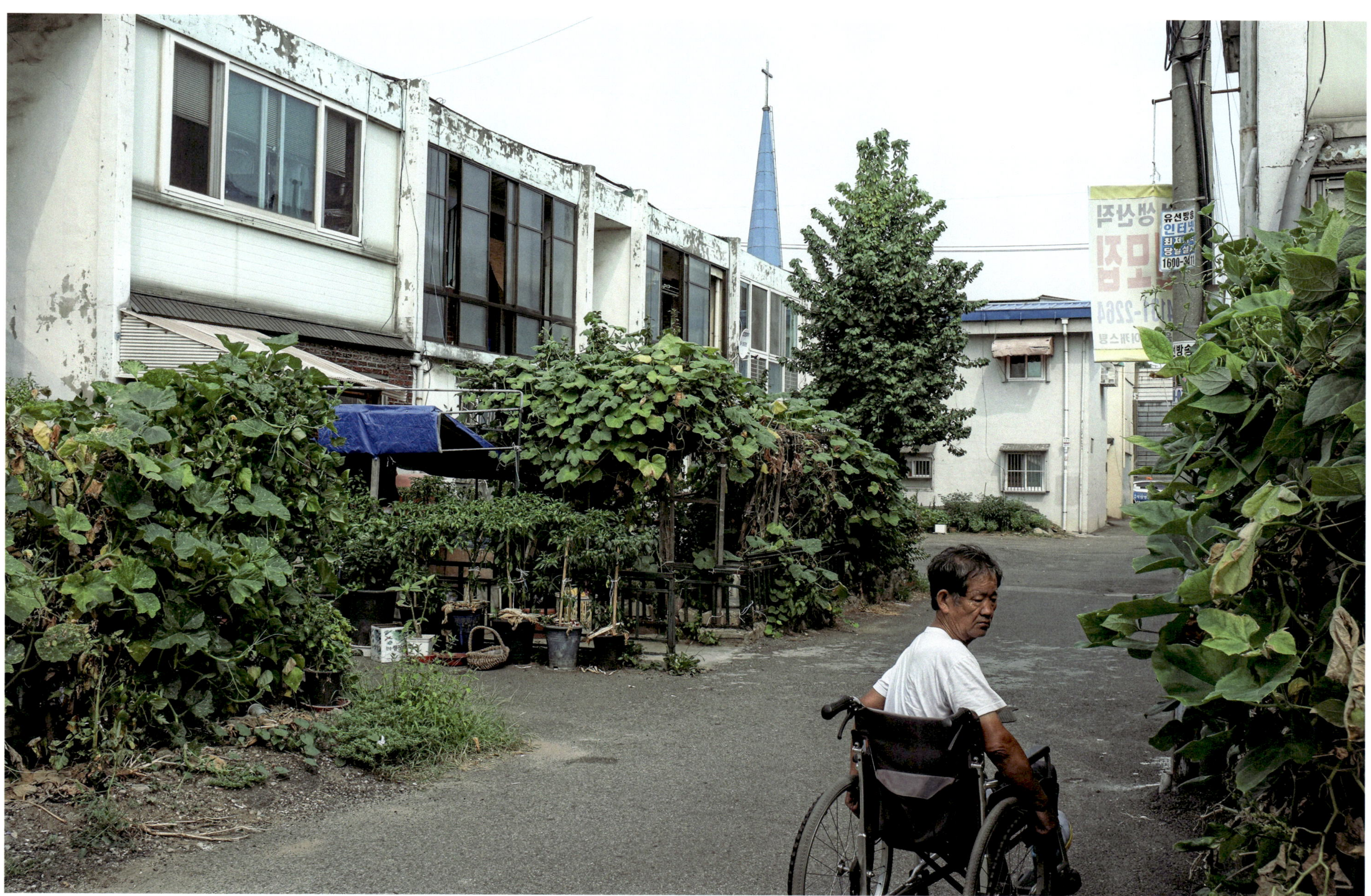

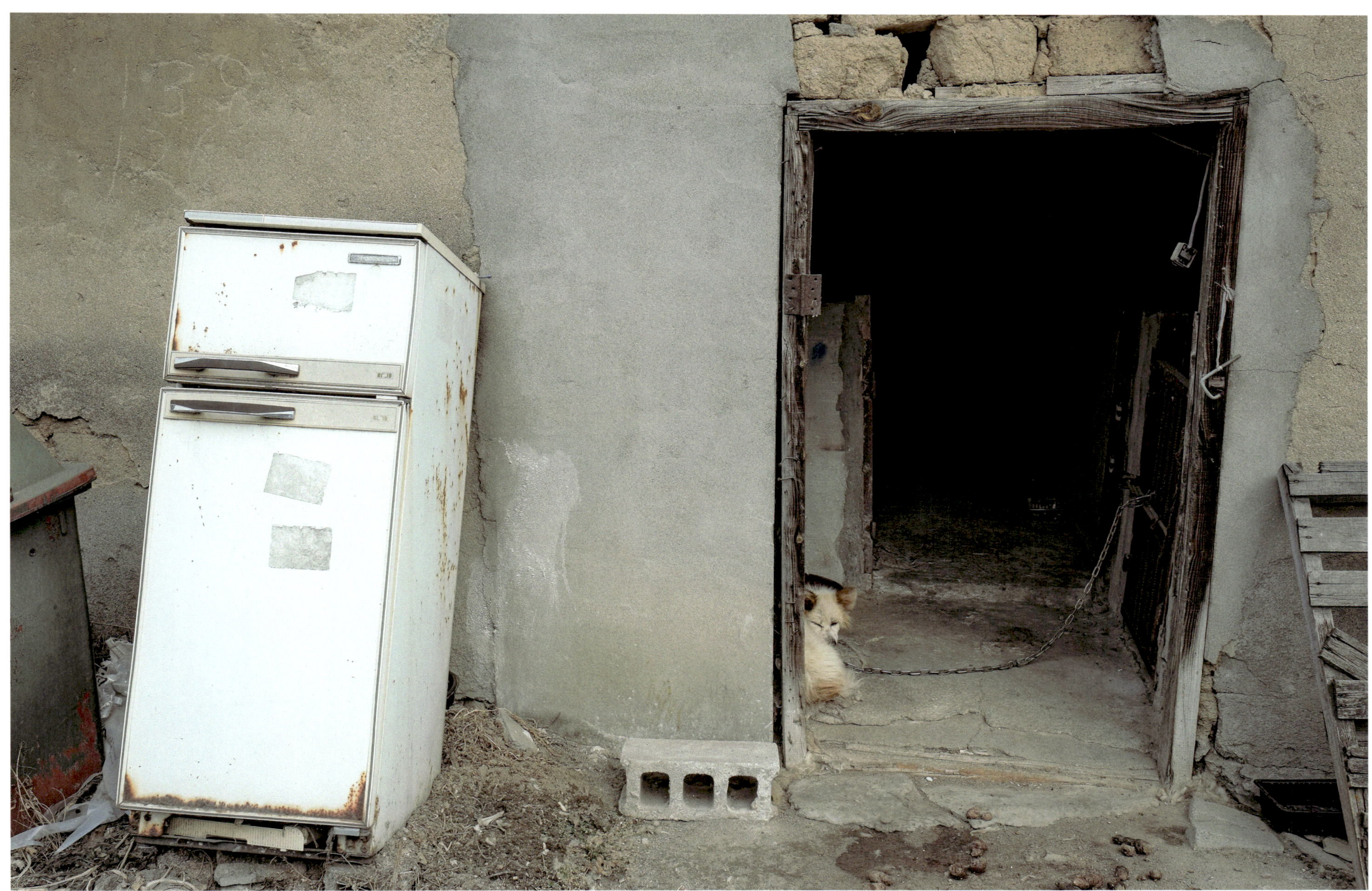

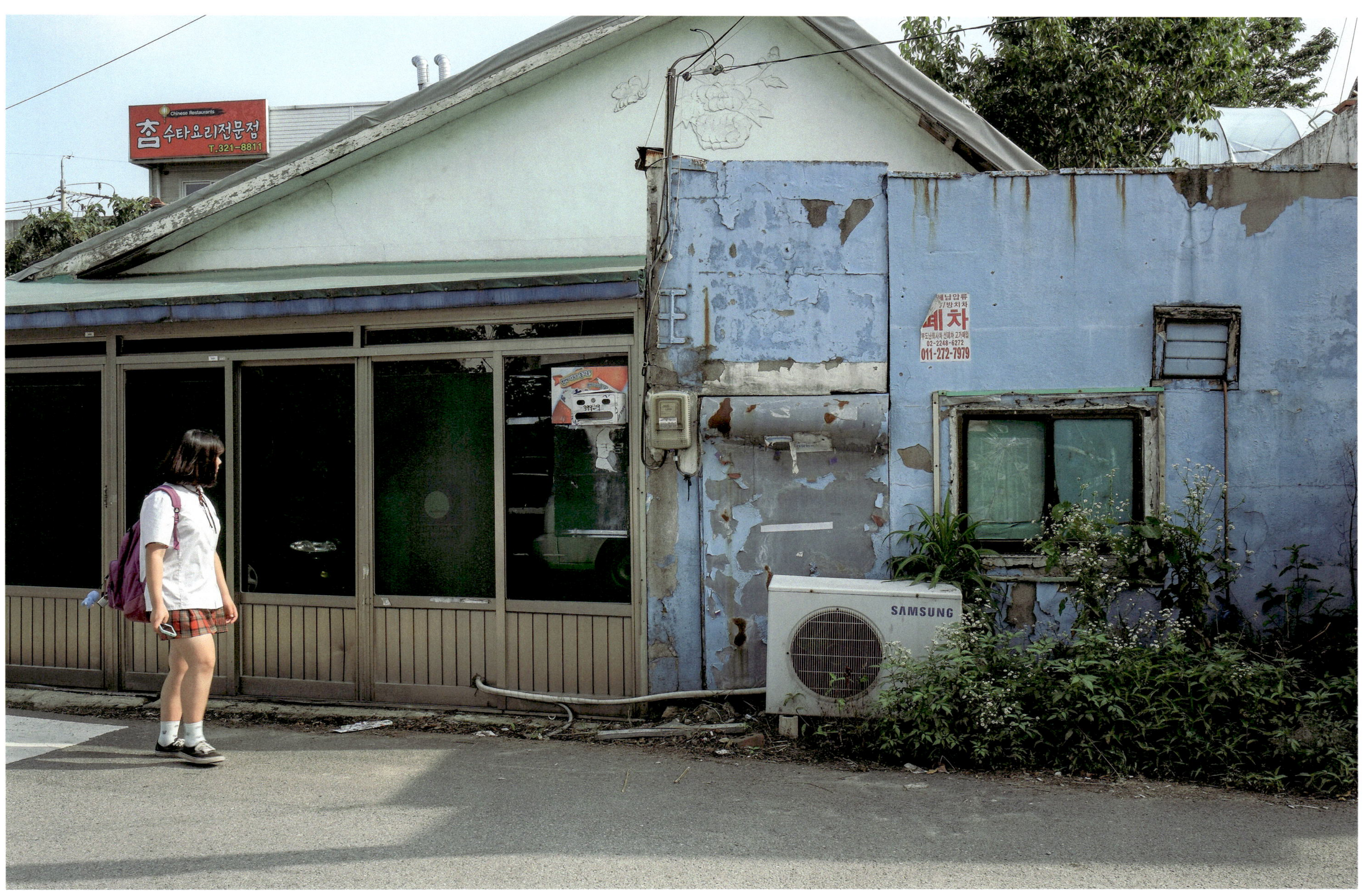
Chinese Restaurants
참 수타요리전문점
T.321-8811
SAMSUNG
예차
02-2248-6272
011-272-7979

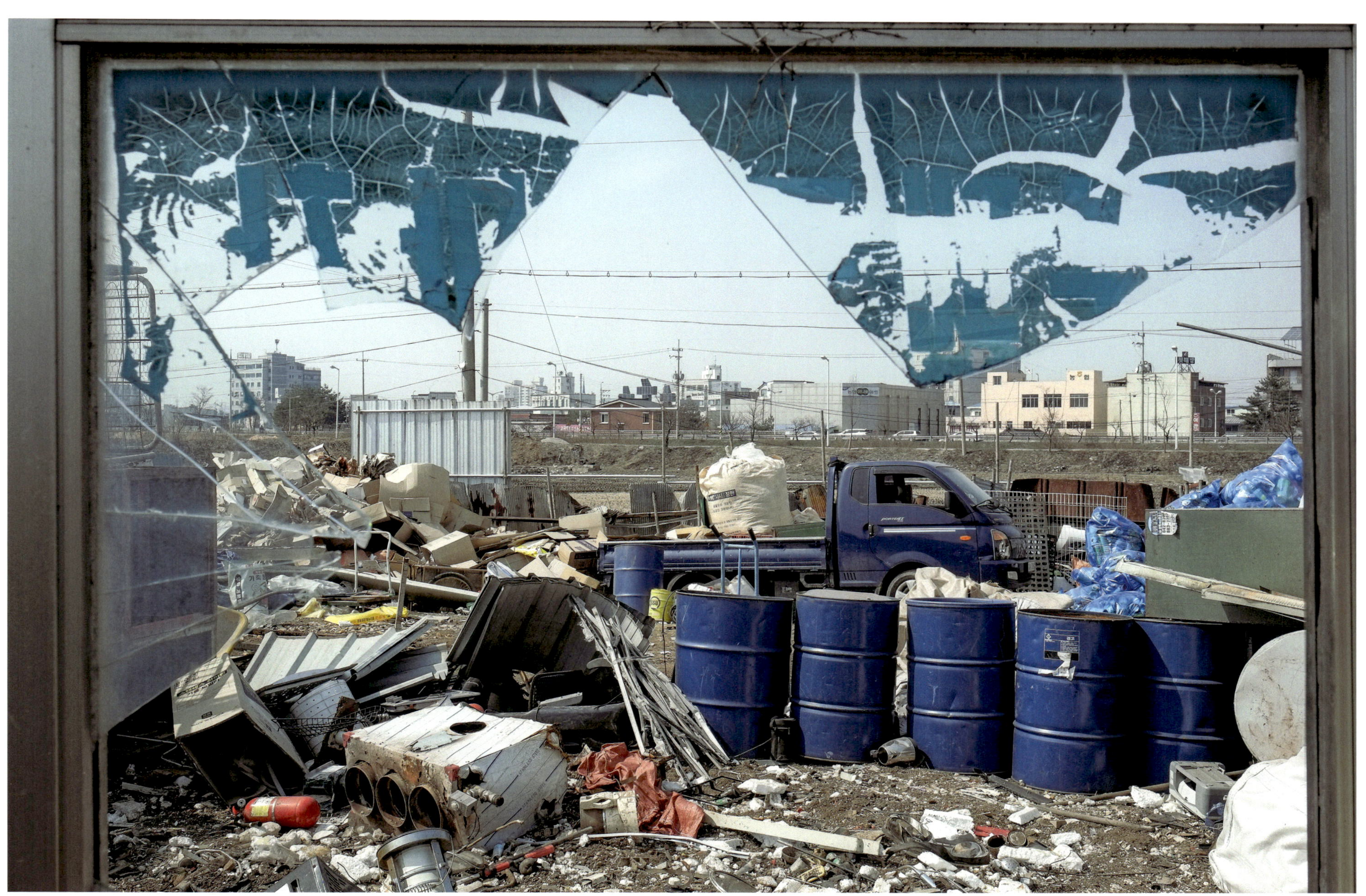

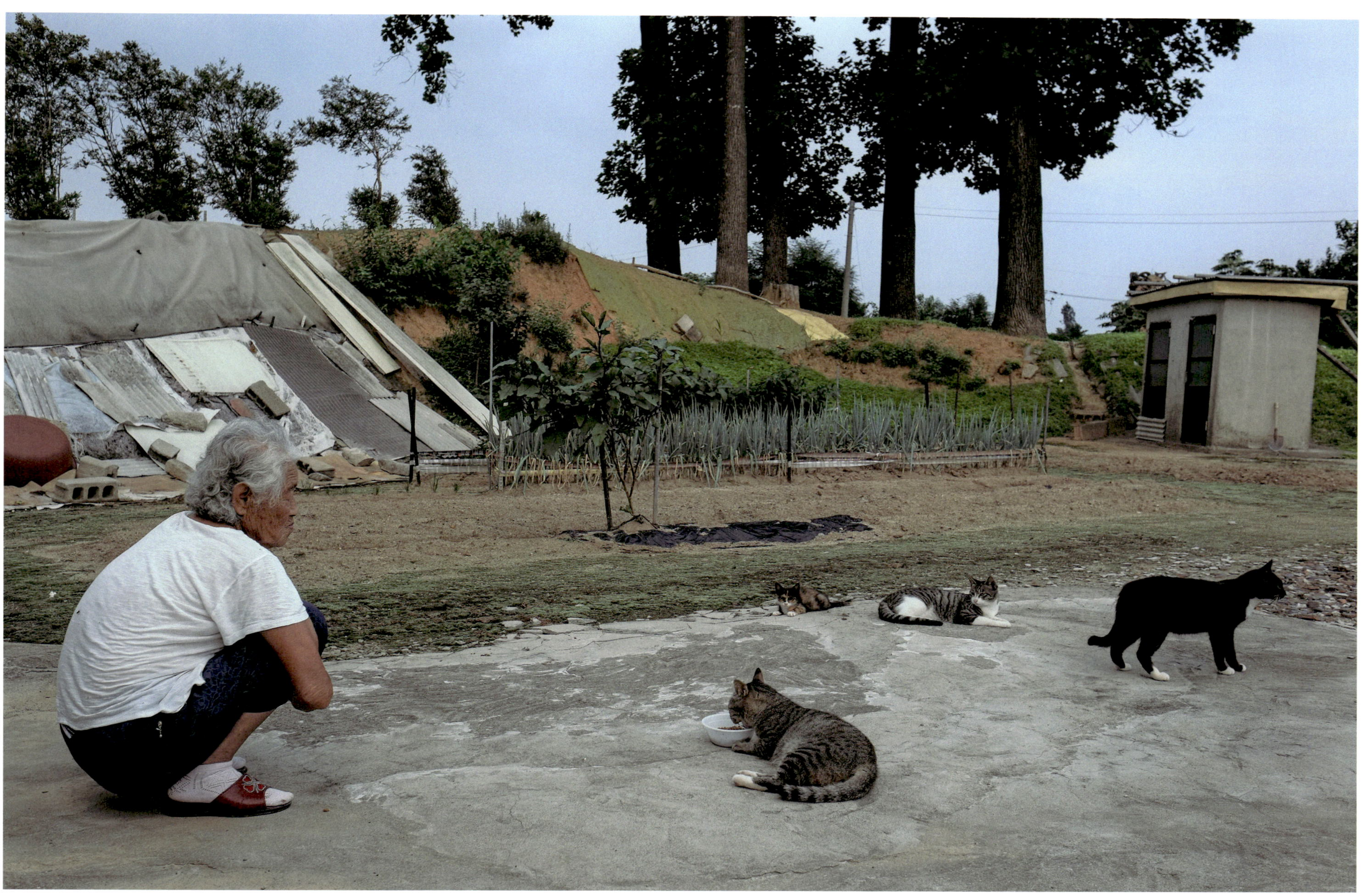

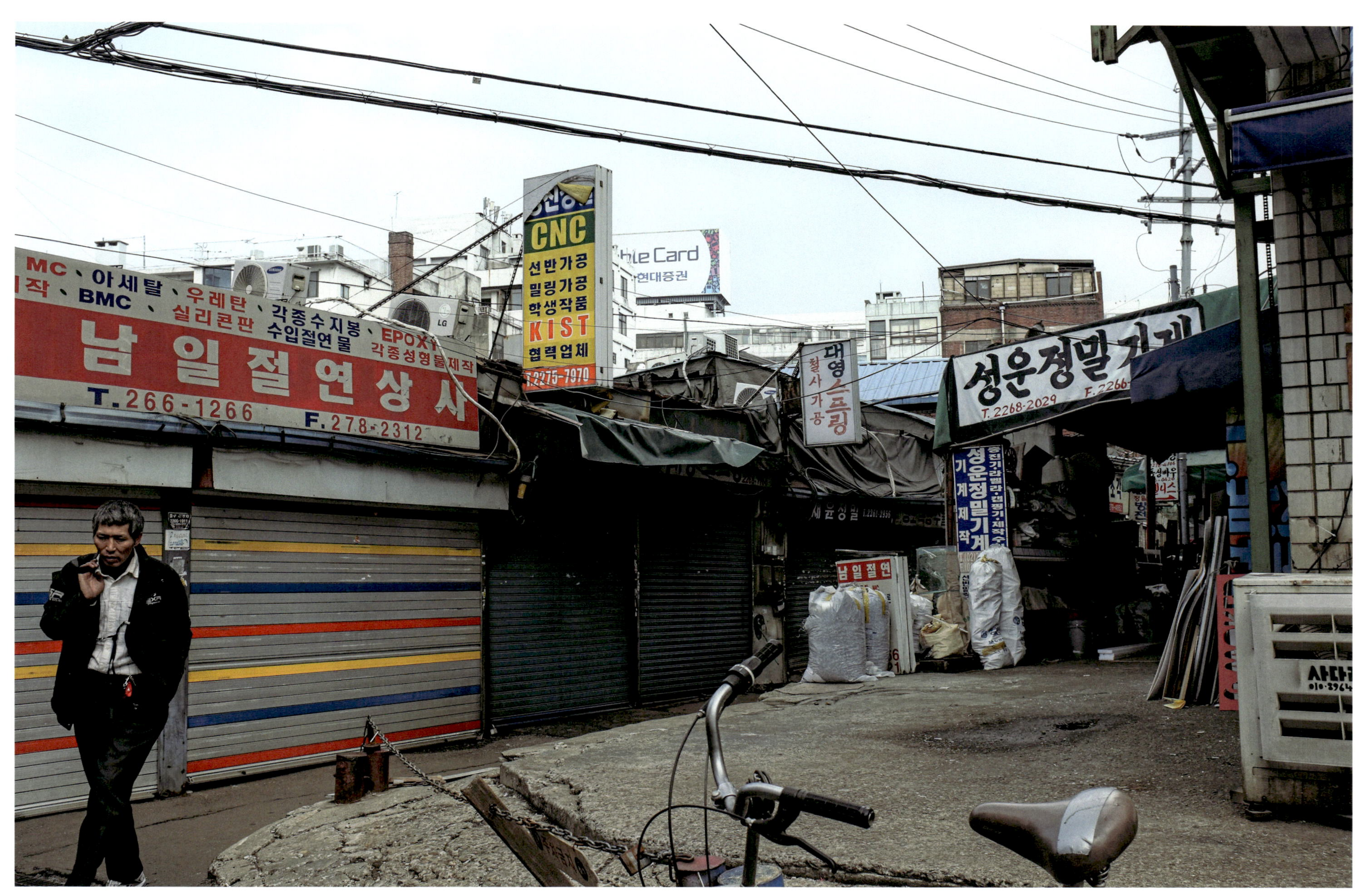

CNC
선반가공
밀링가공
학생작품
KIST
협력업체
T.2275-7970
MC・아세탈・우레탄・각종수지봉・EPOXY
작・BMC・실리콘판 수입절연물 각종성형물제작
남일절연상사
T.266-1266   F.278-2312
대영스프링
활사가공
성운정밀기계
T.2268-2029   F.2266
성운정밀
기계제작
남일절연
사다리

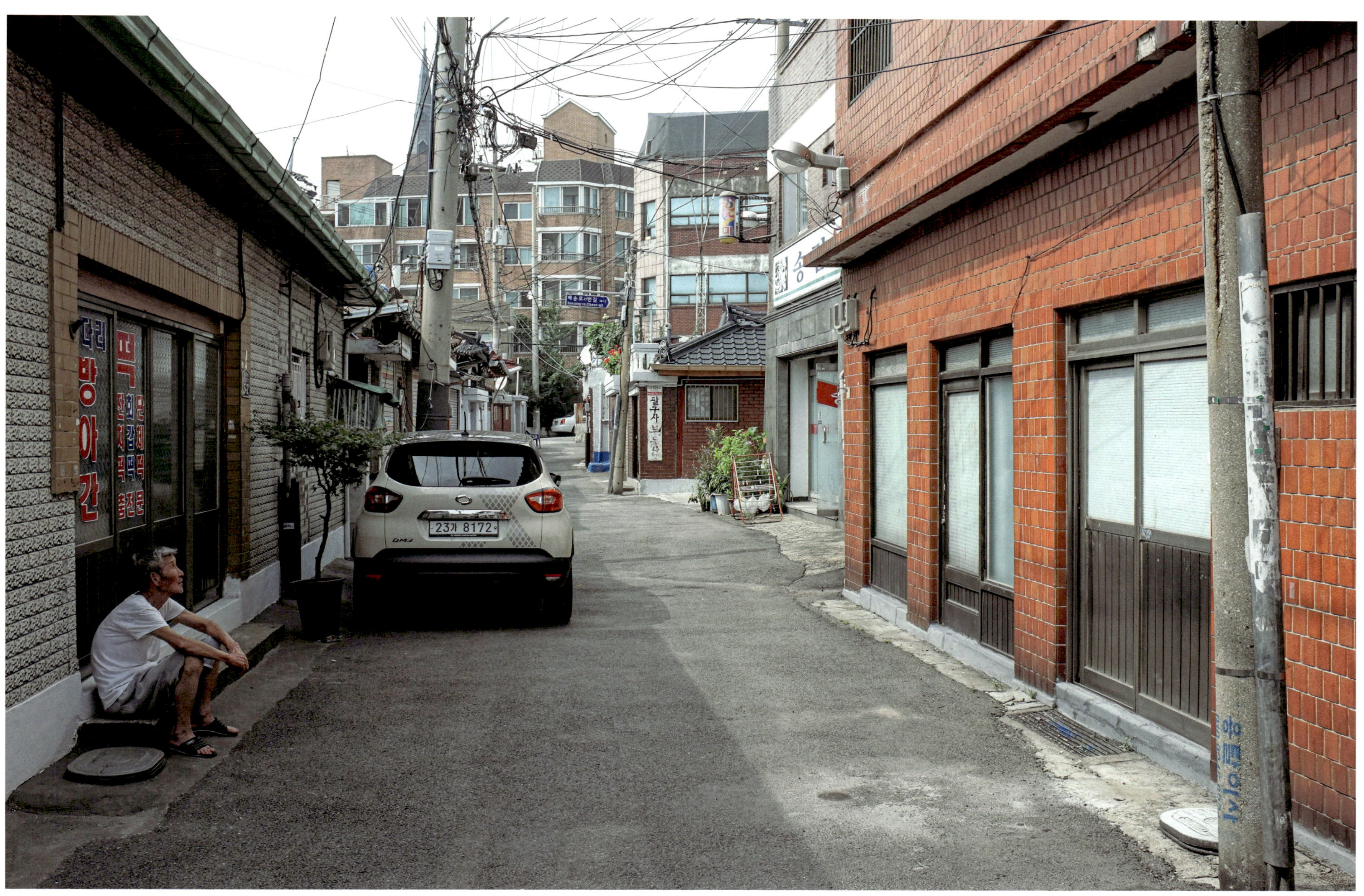

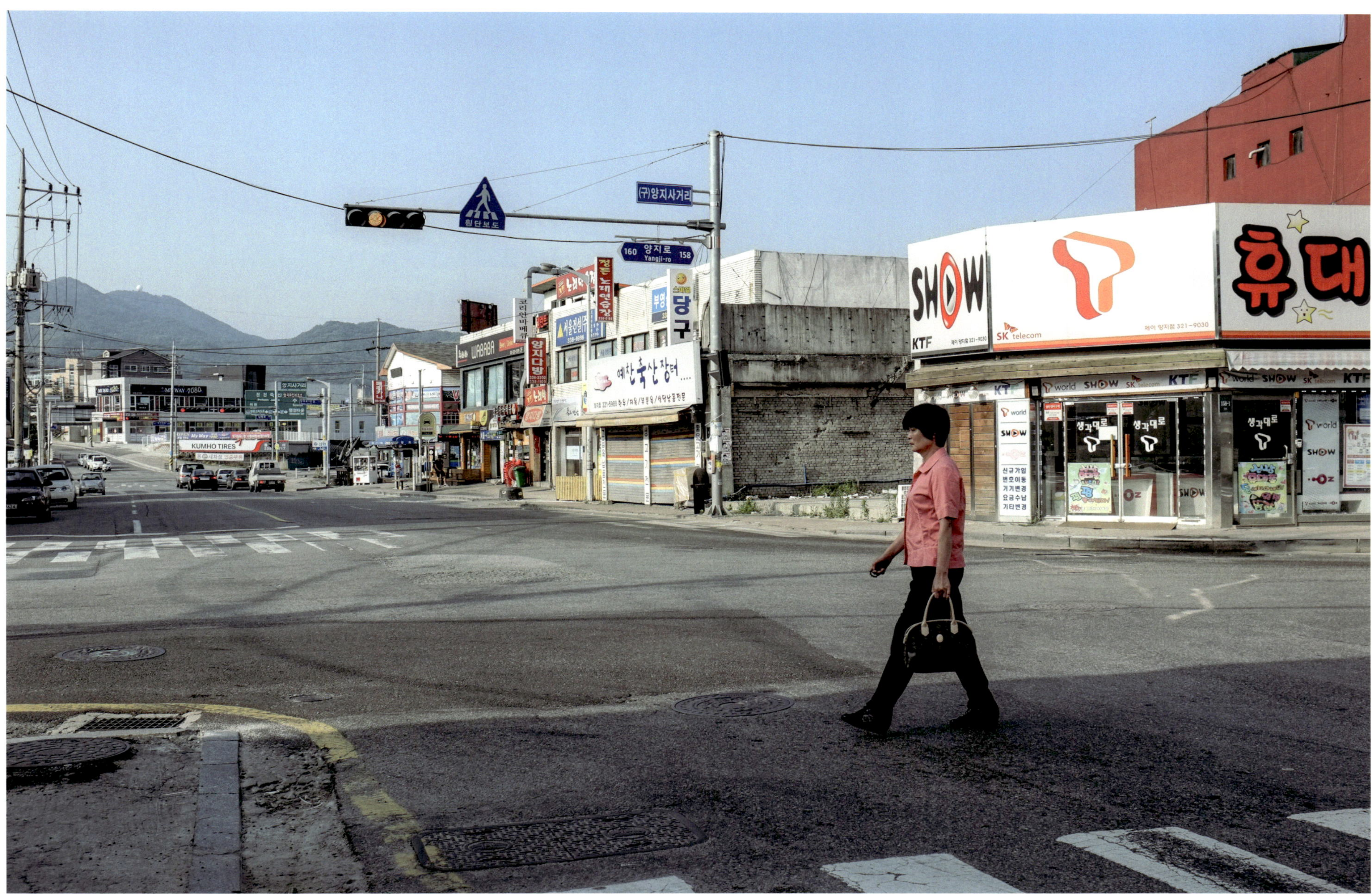

(구)양지사거리
횡단보도
160 양지로 158
Yangji-ro
SHOW
KTF
SK telecom
휴대
생과대로
생과대로
T world
SHOW
SK Telecom
KTF
OZ
신규가입
번호이동
기기변경
요금수납
기타변경
KUMHO TIRES
당구
양지다방
예단축산장터...
WABABA

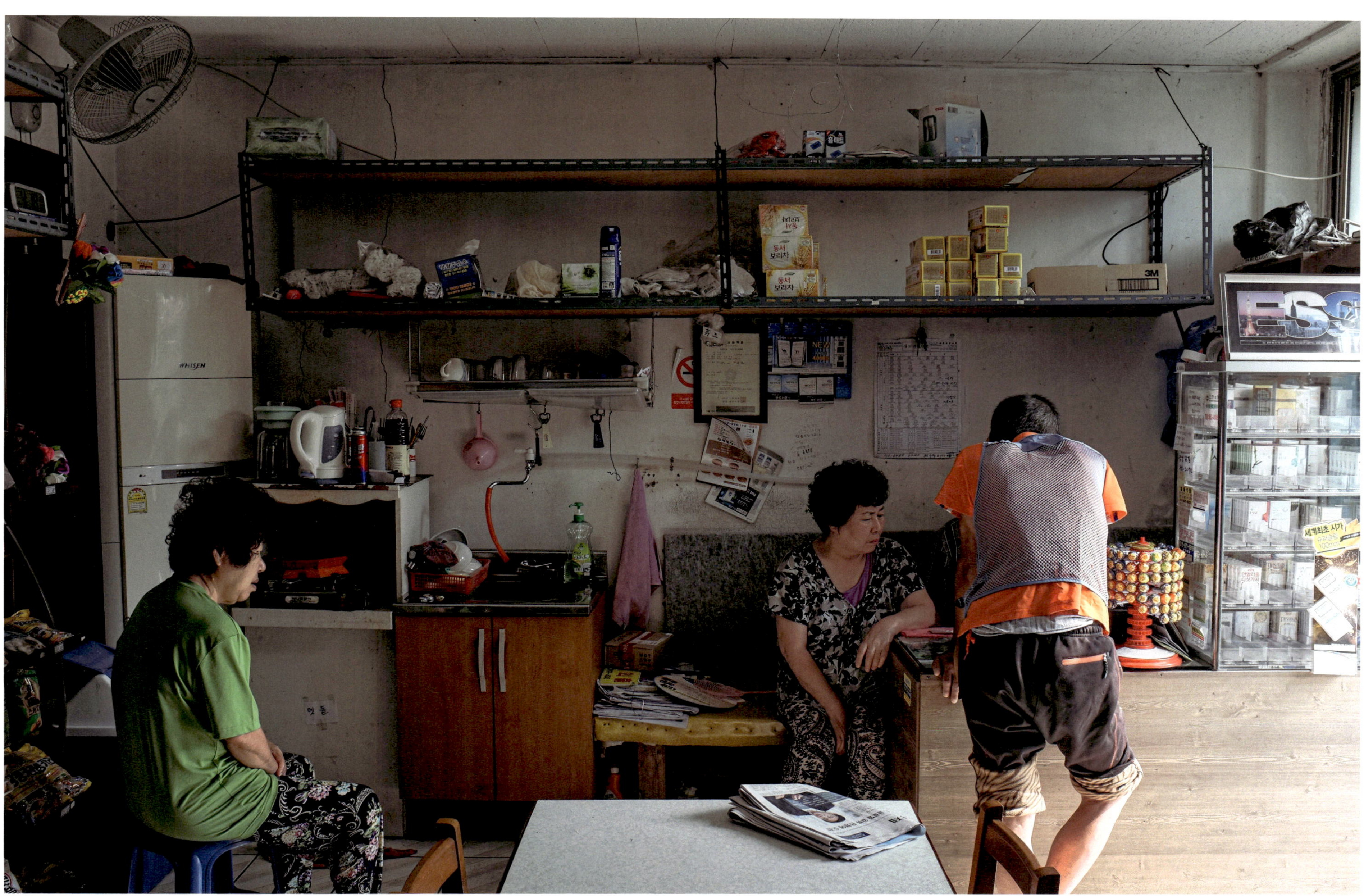

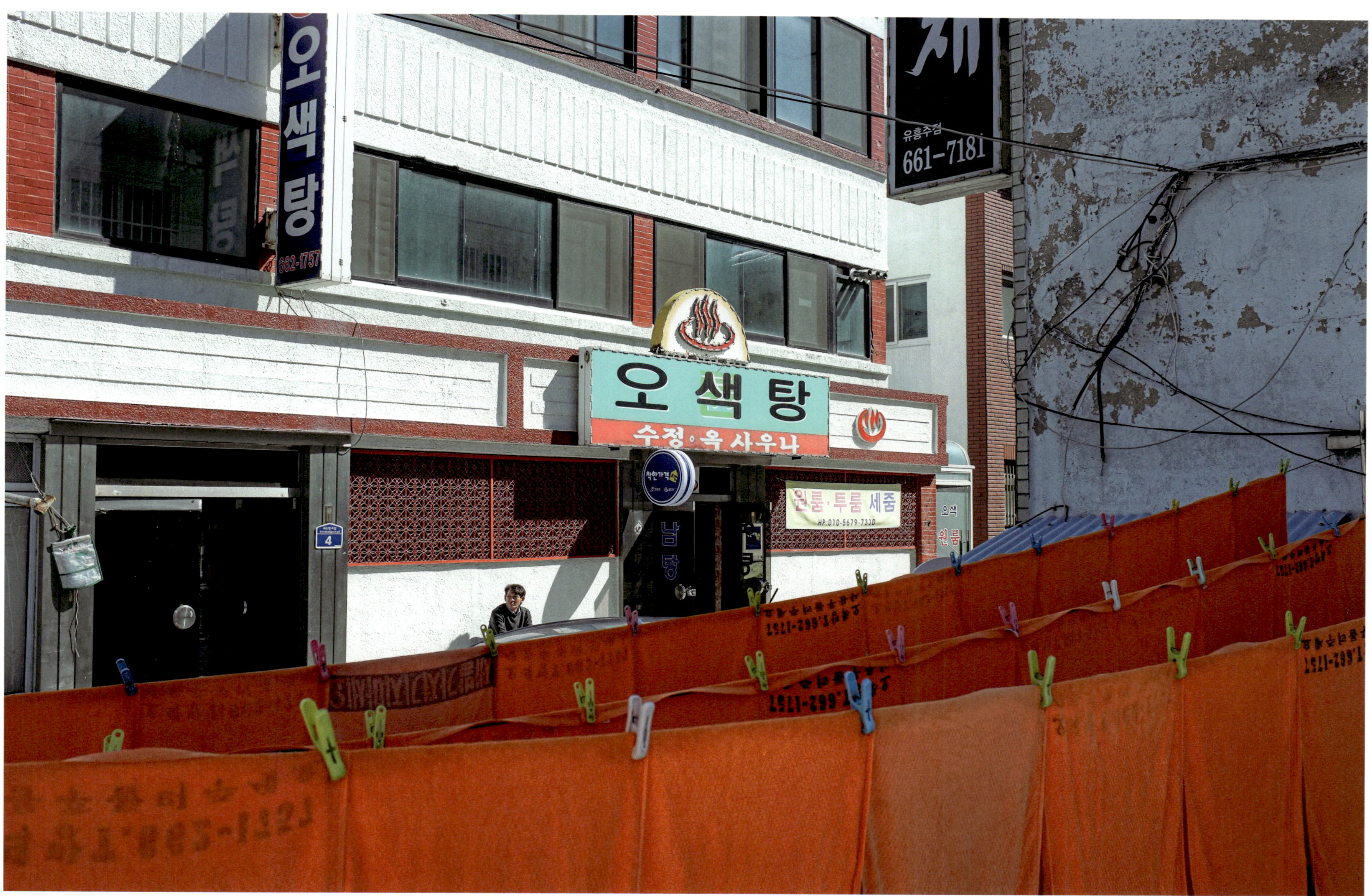

오색탕
662-757
유흥주점
661-7181
제
오색탕
수정·옥 사우나
착한가격
원룸·투룸 세줌
HP.010-5679-7330
오색
원룸
남탕
4

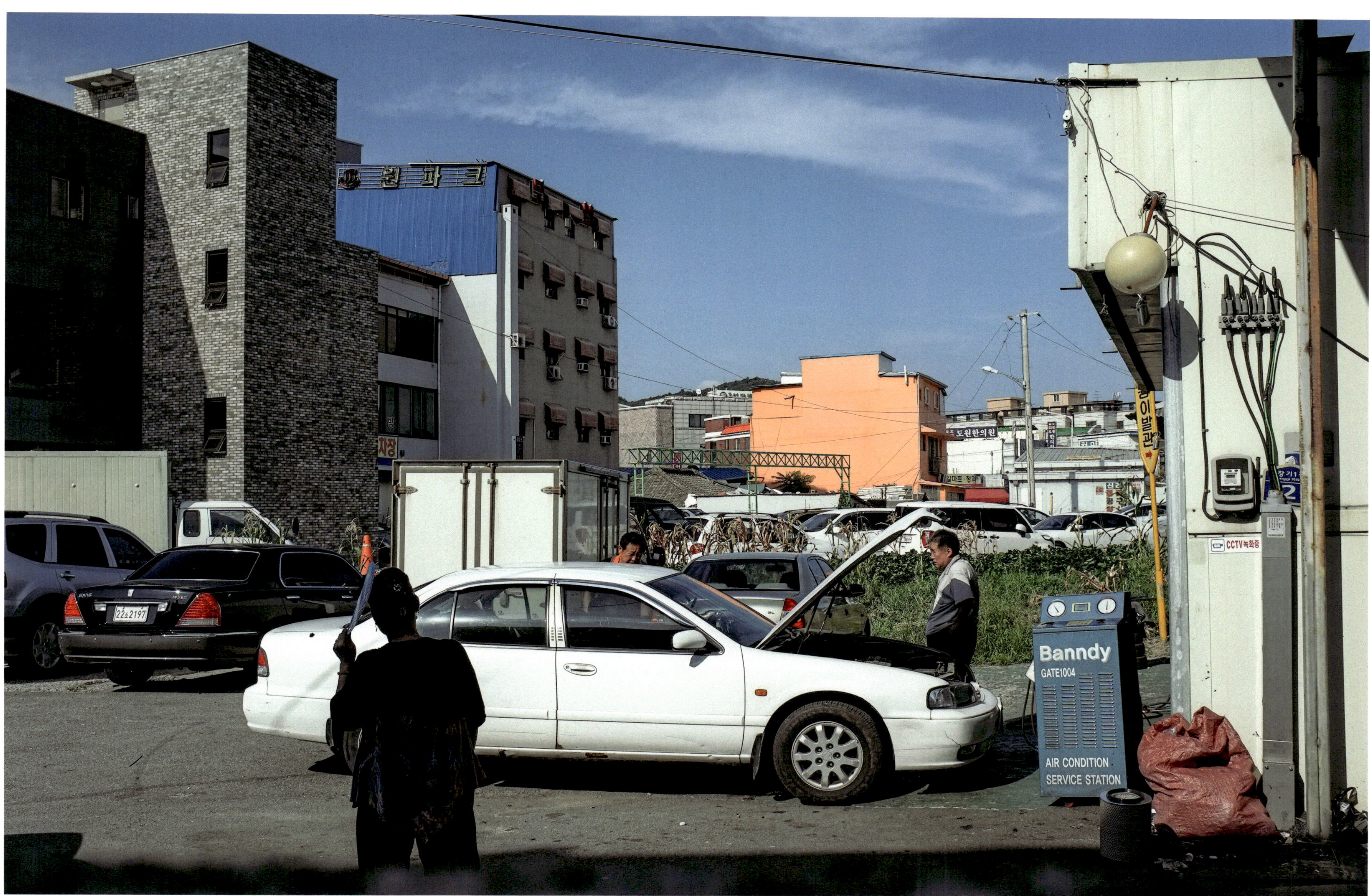

Banndy
GATE1004
AIR CONDITION
SERVICE STATION
CCTV녹화중

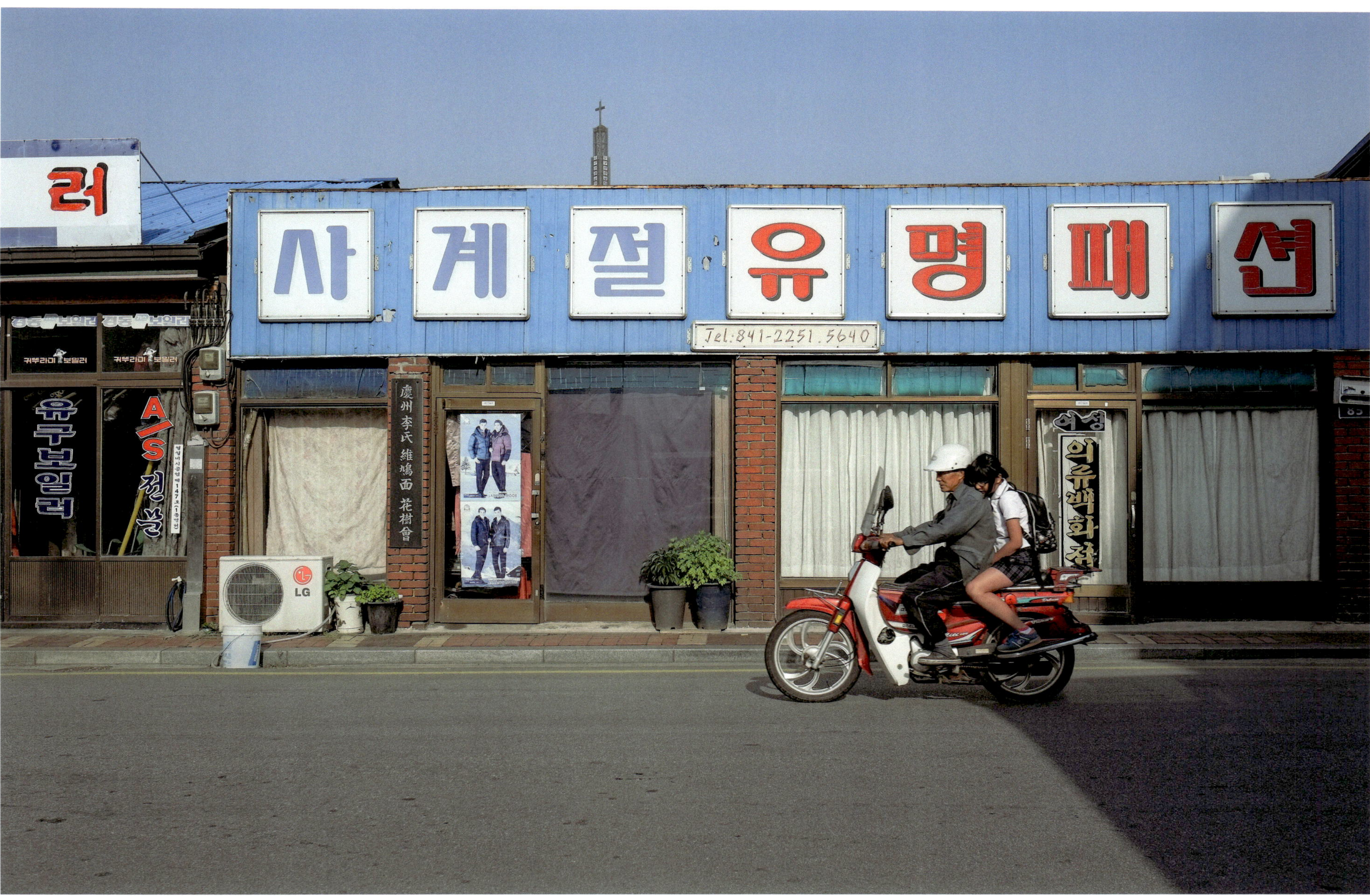

러
사 계 절 유 명 패 션
Tel:841-2251.5640
慶州 李氏 維鳩面 花樹會
유구보일러
A/S 건설
LG
여성
의유백화점

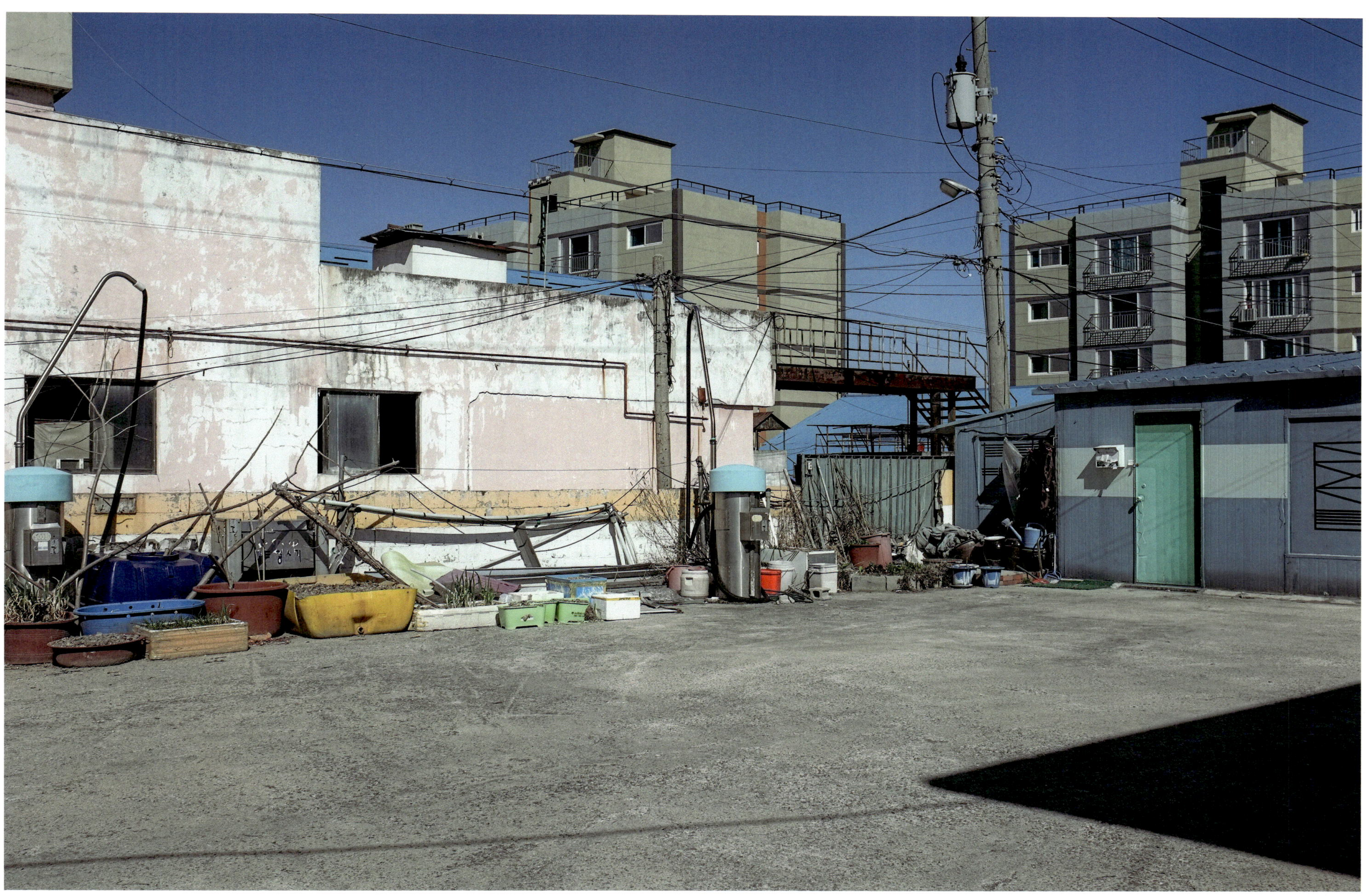

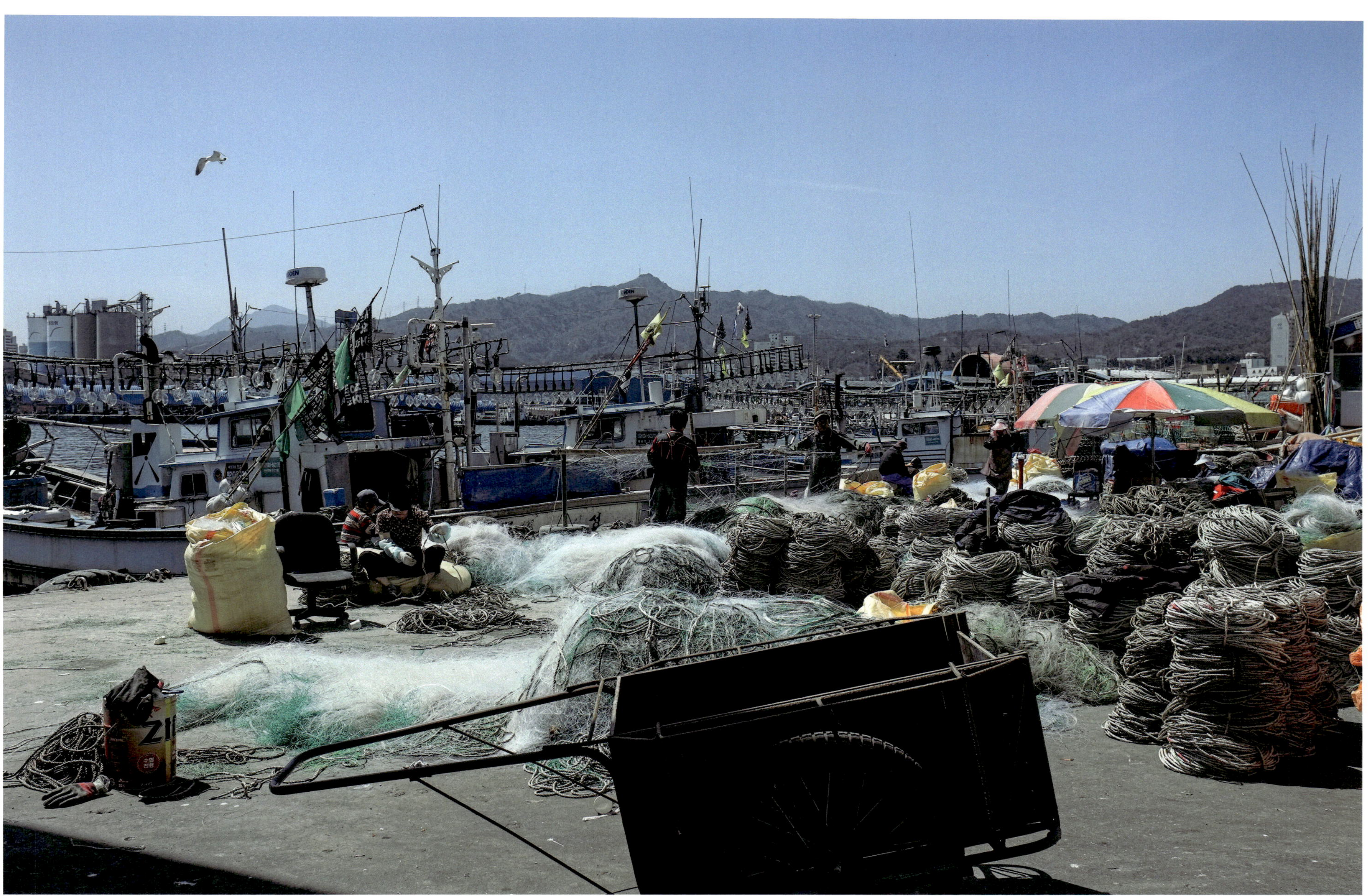

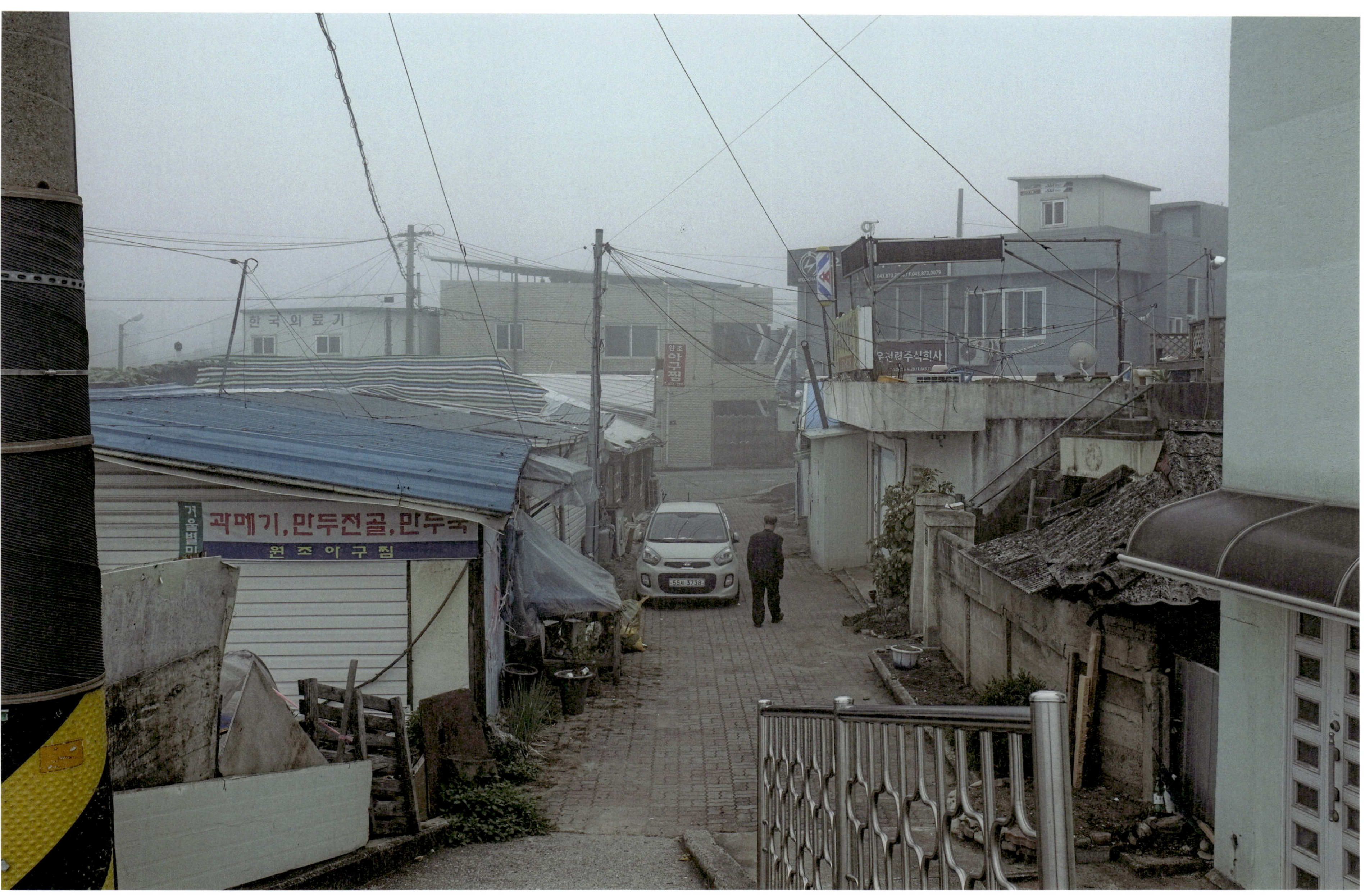
한국의료기
양구찜
한국령주식회사
거울별미
과메기, 만두전골, 만두국
원조아구찜
55보 3738

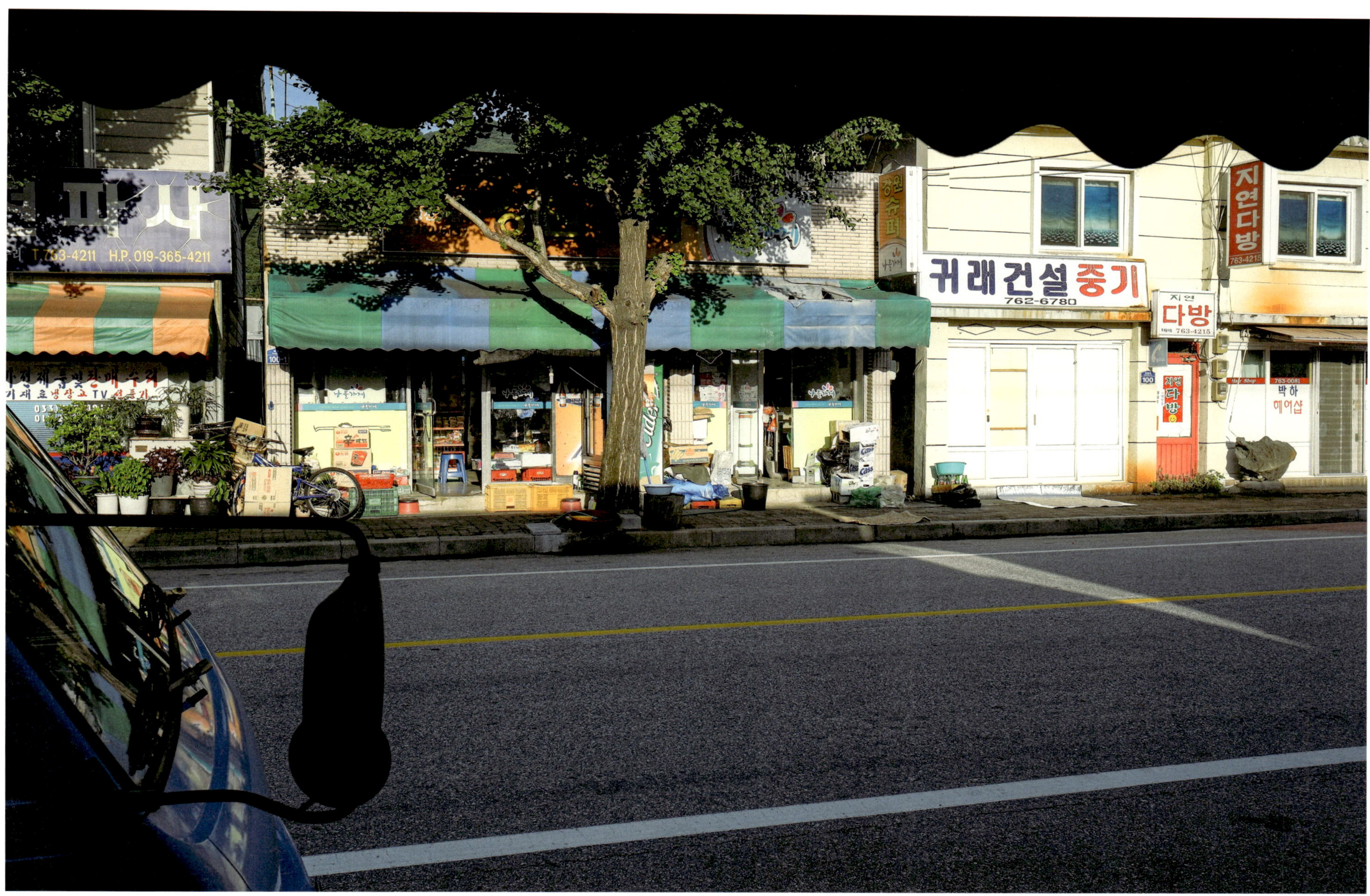
피자
T 763-4211 H.P. 019-365-4211
귀래건설중기
762-6780
지연다방
763-4215
지연
다방
763-4215
100-1
100
박하
헤어샵

Distribution

Switzerland
AVA Verlagsauslieferung
CH – Affoltern am Albis
ava.ch

Germany, Austria
GVA Gemeinsame Verlagsauslieferung
DE – Göttingen
gva-verlage.de

France, Luxembourg, Belgium
Les presses du réel
FR – Dijon
lespressesdureel.com

United Kingdom
Antenne Books
GB – London
antennebooks.com

United States
ARTBOOK / D.A.P.
USA – New York
artbook.com

Japan
twelvebooks
JP – Tokyo
twelve-books.com

Australia, New Zealand
Perimeter Distribution
AU – Melbourne
perimeterdistribution.com

Rest of the world
Edition Patrick Frey
CH – Zürich
editionpatrickfrey.com

Photo credits
Jong Won Rhee

Copyediting
Christian M. Schweizer

Proofreading
Eric Rosencrantz

Book design
Adeline Mollard

Printed and bound by
DZA Druckerei zu Altenburg

Paper
Touch White 145g/m²

Cover
F-Color

Font
LL Bradford

First edition
Edition Patrick Frey, 2021

Print run
800 copies

ISBN 978-3-907236-33-8
Printed in Germany

© 2021 photographs
Jong Won Rhee

© 2021 for this edition
Edition Patrick Frey

Edition Patrick Frey
Limmatstrasse 268
CH-8005 Zürich
editionpatrickfrey.com
mail@editionpatrickfrey.ch

Jong Won Rhee
Solitudes of Human Places

A special moment in photographing is the short-lived moment just before shutter release when you are unconsciously moved by something. You try to capture that fleeting moment of emotions flowing through you without fully understanding them.

These pictures try to preserve that moment through the medium of photography, and represent my personal interaction with Korea, where they were taken. I share these short moments of personal emotions and inspiration with you. This unexpected flow of feelings in the instant before releasing the shutter informs my experience with the world and defines who I am as a person.

My sincere thanks to graphic designer Adeline Mollard, editor Christian M. Schweizer, Andrea Kempter and Patrick Frey for bringing these photographs to life in book form.

This book about mutual understanding, fleeting beauty and enduring hope would not have been possible without the unstinting support of the team at Edition Patrick Frey and my parents and my sister.

I hope they'll all share in my happiness about the publication of this book.

Jong Won Rhee